Praise for GET REAL

Derek Maul's *Get Real* calls Christian men to step unhesitatingly into the reality of new life in Christ. Like the message it echoes, Derek's book is direct and forthright—we are called to and promised transformation through following Jesus. *Get Real* reminds us that God meets us in the ordinariness of our daily lives and makes all things new through the light of our faith in Christ. And as Derek says, "Faith is reality." This book is a welcome traveling companion as we walk—step-by-step, moment by moment—into the reality God has for each of us.

> **—GREGG HUBBARD**
> Keyboardist/vocalist for country/rock band Sawyer Brown

For men even vaguely interested in a deeper spiritual walk, *Get Real* is the right book at the right time. Derek Maul has a heart for real men dealing with the issues of real life. If you are looking for a great resource that will encourage men and strengthen the family, *Get Real* is right on the money.

> **—MARK MERRILL**
> Founder and president, Family First, a nonprofit organization
> dedicated to strengthening the family
> Host, *Family Minute with Mark Merrill* daily radio program

Derek Maul has written a refreshingly honest book that provides a new angle of vision on the quest for a deeper spiritual life. He has a flair for expressing profound thoughts in clear and provocative ways.

> **—THOMAS G. LONG**
> Candler School of Theology
> Emory University
> Atlanta, Georgia

GET REAL

A SPIRITUAL JOURNEY FOR MEN

Derek Maul

UPPER ROOM BOOKS®
NASHVILLE

GET REAL: A Spiritual Journey for Men
Copyright © 2007 Derek Maul
All rights reserved.

The Upper Room Web site: www.upperroom.org

At the time of publication all Web sites referenced in this book were valid. However, due to the fluid nature of the Internet, some addresses may have changed or the content may no longer be relevant.

Unless otherwise indicated, scripture quotations are from the New Revised Standard Version Bible, copyright 1989, Division of Christian Education of the National Council of the Churches of Christ in the United States of America. Used by permission. All rights reserved.

Scripture quotations marked NIV are taken from the HOLY BIBLE, NEW INTERNATIONAL VERSION® (NIV)®. Copyright 1973, 1978, 1984 by International Bible Society. Used by permission of Zondervan. All rights reserved.

Cover design: Left Coast Design, Portland, Oregon
Cover image: Getty/BLOOMimage
Interior design: Gore Studio, Inc./www.GoreStudio.com
First printing: 2007

Library of Congress Cataloging-in-Publication
Maul, Derek, 1956–
    Get real : a spiritual journey for men / Derek Maul.
        p. cm.
    ISBN-13: 978-0-8358-9911-6
    ISBN-10: 0-8358-9911-X
    1. Men—Religious life. 2. Spiritual formation. I. Title.
        BV4528.2.M3246 2006
        248.8'42—dc22

                                                            2006030000

Printed in the United States of America

To my wife, Rebekah,
who has taught me what it means to
live without reservation;

to our children, Andrew and Naomi,
who have helped me understand
the extent of love;

and to all the men and women
who have accompanied me thus far
on the journey.

Author's note regarding language

Many contemporary Christian writers work hard to eliminate gender-exclusive language in reference to God. I respect such inclusive trends, and I believe it's important that Christian scholarship abandon the imprecise practice of limiting God to masculine metaphors. Scripture offers a variety of rich images of the divine, including father, mother, creator, teacher, judge, counselor, warrior, and lover. The divine is even portrayed, on more than one occasion, as a chicken! "How often have I desired to gather your children together as a hen gathers her brood under her wings" (Luke 13:34).

God is clearly understood as much more than exclusively male: "So God created humankind in his image, in the image of God he created them; male and female he created them" (Gen. 1:27). Yet at the same time there is no arguing the evidence that Jesus Christ was 100-percent guy. There is also no disputing the fact that the Bible frequently uses masculine pronouns. This book, then—in respecting the authority of scripture and in specifically addressing our invitation as Christian men to follow Jesus—employs references to God that do not always toe the politically correct line.

We are made in God's image—both male and female—and it's my deep hope and prayer that all people will make the decision to follow Jesus. The lexicon we use when we talk about God (language rooted in this world and limited by time and space) will always be inadequate; it can't be helped. I don't intend to compound the difficulty by compromising my presentation of God through tame, tentative, or nebulous word selection.

CONTENTS

Preface   Treasure in a Clay Jar   9

Introduction   Immersed in the Journey   11

Chapter 1   Good News for Men!   17
Chapter 2   A Round Dozen Flat-out Guys   25

DESIRE

Chapter 3   Where's Our Treasure?   33
Chapter 4   Setting Our Minds on the Things of the Spirit   43

DISCIPLESHIP

Chapter 5   The Structure of a Well-Grounded Faith   53
Chapter 6   Learning to Improvise   61
Chapter 7   Finding a Band of Brothers   71

DEVOTION

Chapter 8   The Long, Deep Breath   81
Chapter 9   To Know Jesus Is to Love Him   89
Chapter 10   Jesus' Prayer and Our Decision to Love   99
Chapter 11   Honest to God   111

DARING

Chapter 12   What Do We Dare?   119
Chapter 13   Living as if Faith Actually Makes a Difference   127
Chapter 14   So What's Stopping Us?   135

Acknowledgments   139

Notes   141

About the Author   143

PREFACE

Treasure in a Clay Jar

We have this treasure in clay jars, so that it may be made clear that this extraordinary power belongs to God and does not come from us. We are afflicted in every way, but not crushed; perplexed, but not driven to despair; persecuted, but not forsaken; struck down, but not destroyed; always carrying in the body the death of Jesus, so that the life of Jesus may also be made visible in our bodies.

—*2 Corinthians 4:7-10*

I am a very ordinary guy. It's important to get that fact out in the open at the onset. Why? Because this book is about extraordinary power, the power to live a life of fullness and abundance, the power to be Christlike in our everyday lives. But I, in and by myself, am simply a clay jar. Anything I do or say that shines, any luminosity that comes from my living, I'm telling you up front that the light—if you can see it at all—has got to be nothing but God.

Which is funny when I think about how I have always dreamed of being an epic spiritual champion. Growing up my heroes were folk like reformed gang member Nicky Cruz of *The Cross and the Switchblade* fame; missionaries David Livingstone, William Carey, and Eric Liddell; and luminary figures in the world of contemporary faith such as Billy Graham, Corrie ten Boom, and British pop icon Cliff Richard.

I remember reading stories of courage and conviction. People who suffered terribly for their faith in concentration camps and gulags, Christ followers who trekked through dark jungles, missionaries who landed airplanes in remote locations, sports and entertainment figures who experienced dramatic conversions. I wanted to have those kinds of stories to tell.

But how on earth would my comfortable life in suburbia with loving parents and a nurturing church family translate into the dramatic stories I imagined?

"Finding Christ after a life of hatred and crime."

"Years of communism and atheism finally yield to God's transforming love."

"International soccer star credits assist to God."

"When we set sail for Africa, I had no idea that a shipwreck would lead to ten years as a pirate. Eventually I met Jesus on the remote island where I was abandoned to my fate."

My imagination knew no bounds. As a child I often lay awake, carefully constructing complex scenarios of personal glory that led to grand testimonies on the stages of great crusades. People would see my life as fascinating and amazing, and they would listen to me with wonder, agog with rapt attention. Generously—in my imagination—I graciously allowed God some supplementary exposure via my generous light.

Around age thirty I remember looking at my life and suddenly realizing that I was a schoolteacher, comfortably married with two children, content in my suburban home. I attended church every Sunday, drove fairly close to the speed limit, watched too much television, and paid my taxes. I had never been in trouble; everyone knew me as kind and easygoing. To tell you the truth, I was a little disappointed in myself.

Then I realized this awesome truth, an understanding that has been growing in me for many years now, the revelation that "We have this treasure in clay jars, so that it may be made clear that this extraordinary power belongs to God and does not come from us." My ordinariness, it turns out, happens to be the perfect vehicle for the glory of God. This is where we live, this world of work and marriage and television and children and church. This is also the exact venue where God purposes to shine. Our ordinariness is God's opportunity.

Spiritual growth or faith formation, then—our deliberate progress as Christians living out our day-to-day lives—is the ultimate exercise in "keeping it real." This is the moment-by-moment story of how we respond to God's love and grace. It is the chronicle of how, in effect, we allow Jesus to be glorified in us.

As Christian men we are called to break out of the mediocrity of uninspired lives. We can achieve such a goal in only one way: we must decide to follow Jesus. Once we engage the process and begin the journey, who knows what manner of testimony we will all have to tell?

INTRODUCTION

Immersed in the Journey

What exactly do I mean when I say that I am a Christian?

[Jesus said] "I am the light of the world. Whoever follows me will never walk in darkness but will have the light of life."

—*John 8:12*

Once we have made the decision to set the whole process in motion—in the context of a deliberate choice to believe—then we are Christian. The manner in which we engage the journey is the story of our discipleship.

—Get Real, *page 15*

For the past several years I have written a weekly op-ed column that runs in several Tampa area newspapers. Regular readers understand that my observations and commentary are fundamentally shaped by my perspective as a Christian man. I try to present a viewpoint that references the bedrock of faith central to my thinking and my writing.

But what exactly does it mean to be a Christian in today's world? Ask three different people, and you may well hear three different answers. The truth of the matter—even though the saving grace of Jesus must always be the touchstone—is that we don't always find ourselves reading from the same page when it comes to communicating the message.

Fact is, there's a great deal of misinformation circulating nowadays regarding what it really means to be a Christian living in the twenty-first century. Along with misinformation comes confusion. Simply put, I don't want people to be confused about Jesus.

Unfortunately, the fringe element and misleading representations of Christianity tend to generate the most airtime. When televangelists call for international assassinations or spiritual leaders condemn entire municipalities to God's vengeance, we can be sure to see footage all over the nightly news. Everyone in America knows the details when figures like televangelist Jim Bakker go down in flames. The press loves to quote some of the more controversial clerics when they insist they represent God's exact opinion regarding who to vote for or what causes we should support politically. The media have a field day when some preacher in Kansas suggests that God deliberately sent AIDS to reduce the homosexual population. Whole communities are privy to the sordid facts when a minister has an affair or misappropriates funds. And even when they stay out of trouble, a lot of Christian leaders manage to garner media attention by casting the spotlight on legalism, condemnation, chauvinism, and petty prejudices.

I often shake my head in wonder and think about the timeless advice of Francis of Assisi (1182–1226). Saint Francis suggested that we all focus on preaching the gospel simply through the way we live, and that we only resort to using words when absolutely necessary.

But we live in a loud and highly opinionated society, and some of the most strident voices prove to be the least mindful of the standard Saint Francis put forward.

In 2002 Alabama Supreme Court Chief Justice Roy Moore went to great lengths to place a huge slab of rock in his courthouse. The monument featured the Ten Commandments. Many Christians rallied around the judge in the ensuing controversy, and several of the protesters presented themselves and the gospel as obnoxious and boorish. Such behavior merely served to further convince an enormous audience that the story of salvation as presented has little to say to them in the way of peace, relevance, personal victory, or reconciliation.

By the time the controversy died down, most people had missed one of the more interesting facts: the recalcitrant judge had his behemoth placard chiseled in old King James English, and its meaning was all but lost on those who most needed the message. Additionally, the majority of the protests had more to do with politics than with demonstrating God's remarkably relevant love to an extraordinarily needy world.

If I had a couple of hundred thousand dollars to spend and some public place to display a big rock, I believe I'd more likely choose to inscribe a verse like Micah 6:8: "He has told you, O mortal, what is good; and what does the Lord require of you but to do justice, and to love kindness, and to walk humbly with your God?" Or maybe Christ's beatitudes from Matthew 5, or even this simple phrase that Jesus shared with his disciples: "As the Father has loved me, so I have loved you; abide in my love" (John 15:9).

Here's the bottom line: We can drag multiton slabs of rock into places guaranteed to foster controversy and force debate regarding the merits of religious displays in public buildings, or we can live eloquent and humble lives of faith. To me, the preference is obvious.

Christianity as politics

Some people go to great lengths to insist that the Christian faith is interchangeable with "traditional" North American mores, patriotism, political conservatism, "family values," or some of the more extreme positions that define right-wing ideology. Such approaches involve a lot of legalism and leave little room for discussion. I recently spoke with a man who insisted—with all sincerity—that he had never known a Democrat who was also a Christian. He was genuinely surprised that such an anomaly might even exist!

When a situation like this occurs, the teachings of Christ are in effect subsumed into a set of cultural and political postulates regarding correct behavior, belief, ideals, and opinions—positions that are then presented as "God's way." Not only is this message typically closed to dialogue, but it comes fully loaded with condemnation for those who dare to dissent.

Christianity as an experience

Other believers describe Christianity in stereotypical and subjectively experiential terms. One moment you are not a Christian, then the next, something sudden and overwhelming happens. "Abracadabra"—there you are, good to go.

A great deal of mystique tends to surround such definitions of Christianity. More often than not an emotional experience of comparable quality and intensity is required for acceptance into the "in" crowd. The authenticity of a believer's spiritual pedigree can easily be called into question. Indeed, spiritual one-upmanship can run rampant when the perceived quality of an experience becomes the litmus test for sanctity or membership in the inner circles of salvation.

Christianity as social behavior

Yet a third approach equates *Christian* simply with church membership; being a Christian is somewhat like belonging to a spiritually themed social club. "My parents go there, the other parents at my children's school, most of my bridge club, and a lot of my business contacts too—so of course I'm a Christian." This characterization of Christianity is primarily concerned with social networking, appropriate appearances, cultural rights of passage, and ancillary participation in philanthropic activities. According to this view, Jesus' teachings represent the great philosophy of humankind's deepest yearning—"We're all good people, you know"—and worship is merely a solemn occasion where the community gathers.

But what did Jesus say?

What these and other fashionable understandings of the Christian faith commonly seem to miss are the most essential points that Jesus himself advanced throughout his three years of public speaking and teaching.

Here is what Jesus said just before his ascension, his famous last words to his band of loyal followers: "Go therefore and make disciples of all nations . . . teaching them to obey everything that I have commanded you" (Matt. 28:19-20).

Christ had previously defined discipleship like this: "If you hold to my teaching, you are really my disciples" (John 8:31, NIV) and "By this everyone will know that you are my disciples, if you have love for one another" (John 13:35).

Christ's friends were first called Christians sometime after his death and resurrection. The term *Christian* was coined because it seemed to be the most accurate way to describe the growing number of Christ followers. When people saw Peter, John, James, Andrew, and the other believers, they naturally thought of Jesus. The early Christians reminded people of Jesus because they were, first and foremost, faithful disciples.

If I am a Christian, then, it is because I have made a deliberate decision to follow Christ. It means I have accepted the wonderful truth that because of Christ's life, death, and resurrection, I am now made right with God. Additionally, it means I am taking the necessary steps to become a disciplined student of Christ's teachings and his way.

I have, in short, immersed myself in the journey.

In his famous conversation with Nicodemus, Jesus described the process of reorienting ourselves to God's way as being "born of the Spirit" (John 3:6). Because being born of the Spirit is such a radical departure from the path we are naturally inclined to take, it is a lot like completely starting over.

Once we have made the decision to set the whole process in motion—in the context of a deliberate choice to believe—then we are Christian. The manner in which we engage the journey is the story of our discipleship.

In John 3:16-17 Jesus points out the following: "For God so loved the world that he gave his only Son, so that everyone who believes in him may not perish but may have eternal life. Indeed, God did not send the Son into the world to condemn the world, but in order that the world might be saved through him."

The mystery of Christianity is the manner in which God works powerfully to be with us in response to our ongoing commitment to follow his way.

The Christian life is not about political ideology, or about condemnation, or about trumping someone else's experience. It is about Jesus, about being his disciple, about falling in love with God, and about having the courage to let that kind of devotion actually change your life.

This is what I mean when I say that I am a Christian writer. There is little I can say outside of that perspective that will mean anything at all in the final analysis.

The life of a Christian man

The Christian life is not about political ideology, or about condemnation, or about trumping someone else's experience.

- It is about Jesus,
- about being his disciple,
- about falling in love with God,
- and about having the courage to let that kind of devotion actually change your life.

1   GOOD NEWS FOR MEN!

In this world you will have trouble. But take heart! I have overcome the world.

—*John 16:33*, NIV

Life, at its core, is essentially uncomplicated. The Christian life is simpler still.

Regrettably, elegant paradigms go against the grain regarding most everything we have been taught as grown-up men. We like to impress ourselves and dazzle one another with extraordinarily complex layers of detail. We tend to pile on absurd complications in response to the misguided notion that significance and validation can be measured in terms of feverish levels of activity. "Look at me," we're inclined to say. "I'm way busier than you. I win!"

Some of us begin each new chapter of our lives by making desperate promises. Sometimes we even draw up a list of resolutions to do better. The checklist may have already begun:

1. Simplify my life
2. Try harder to be a better Christian
3. Read the rest of this book
4. Quit making so many lists . . .

Is it too soon to ask how things are shaping up? Between you and me, I'm not really big on resolutions. When it comes to owning real change in our lives, little proves so unhelpful as one more set of surface-level promises.

Fact is, we often hide behind lists and resolutions because we'd rather not tackle issues of greater depth. It's a lot easier to say, "I swear off donuts" or "I resolve to read more helpful books" or even "I'll say the Lord's Prayer every day" than to deal with the possibility and the risk of transformation. It's a lot less painful emotionally to see ourselves fall off the calorie wagon or fail to improve our reading list than to own up to failures of family, character, faith, or deeply held dreams.

On the other hand, by the very act of choosing trivia, of deliberately keeping our expectations low, we effectively reduce the stakes and avoid the potential pitfalls of challenges that actually mean something. That way we don't have to invest anything that might cost us because there's nothing of value for us to lose or, for that matter, to gain.

Just recently I took some deliberate time to talk over my plans with God. Or to be more honest, I took the opportunity to instruct the Almighty regarding how I imagined he should handle certain matters in my life. It's a direction too many of my prayers tend to take.

I had been searching for answers. I was concerned about the direction of my work, and I felt the need for some kind of sign. So I walked my dog, Mozart, out in the cool, clear evening air and spent a few minutes thinking through the situations in my life.

I love shooting stars. I've always considered them a kind of talisman, and this particular evening was a great one for peering deep into the sky. So I asked God to confirm my prayers with a blaze of light across the dark, clear night.

Nothing happened.

I wondered if maybe the enormous oak trees hanging over the sidewalk were blocking my view, so I dragged my reluctant dog up onto the golf course behind our house. We stationed ourselves in the middle of the seventh green—just to make things easier for God. I looked up at the huge night sky and waited for my sign.

After a while Mozart started looking at me with his best "I'm done; we're both cold, so why are we still standing around?" expression. I was in the middle of explaining to him that we were waiting for God to get up to speed with my definition of communication when a moment of clarity hit me. It was brighter than any meteor streaking through the night sky.

It wasn't as if I could hear an audible voice, but I understood exactly what God was saying. *"Isn't it enough that I hold these billions of stars in the heavens? Now you want me to fling one across the sky just to confirm something you already know!"*

Embarrassed, I quickly conceded the point and experienced a great moment of personal assurance. *"I am with you; I am for you; I believe in you. I believe in your work and fully intend to be a part of this process."*

The attendant sense of understanding continued. *"I simply want you to get it into your head that I expect this level of dialogue at the beginning of every day,"* God explained. *"That way I can be more completely vested in the process of everything you do."*

That was it—no fanfare, no angels, not even the vaguest hint of a shooting star. Not exactly a New Year's resolution, but instead a fresh confirmation of commitment that will surely affect the substance of everything I think, everything I write, everything I say, every detail of my life.

"And remember," Jesus said at the very end of his ministry, "I am with you always, to the end of the age" (Matt. 28:20).

The Men's Room

My firmest spiritual anchor is my discipleship group, known around church as The Men's Room. We meet every Wednesday evening after worship. In addition to Bible study, the group is carefully designed to provide mutual support, encouragement, and—most importantly—accountability in the context of relationship.

Accountability is where the rubber meets the road in The Men's Room. Our covenant states clearly that we can bring anything to the table, and that honesty about our lives and our personal struggles is essential if we plan to make any kind of headway. The companion to honesty is confidentiality. We have learned to trust, and our confidence in one another is ironclad. We share what is on our hearts, look to the scriptures for wisdom and guidance, and our prayers cut to the heart of the matter because we are well past playing games.

We are discovering—together—what it means to be a Christian man in the twenty-first century. Homework is simple: we apply the lessons of Wednesday evening to the daily realities of life, at home and at work, during the week. What we have learned is a powerful testimony to how a well-nurtured spiritual life changes both us and our world.

Nineteen men make up this group: a high school teacher, a retired executive, a medical sales rep, a software engineer, a custodian, a school principal, an airline pilot, a sales manager, a CFO (chief financial officer), a librarian, a retired manager, a public health administrator, a truck driver, a factory worker, an accountant, a writer, an office manager, a manufacturer's representative, and an entrepreneur.

We range in age from thirty to seventy, and among us we have children at various stages of life from age three on up. Eric became a Christian most recently; Gary renewed his faith a couple of years ago; Jerry served as an elder before Brad was even born. Politically we're all over the map, and our social backgrounds are just as varied. We all have one thing in common, however: the desire to grow in faith and to serve God more effectively in this world.

I am writing this book, then, not from theory or speculation but in the certain knowledge that God honors our intention and our honest efforts to know him. I will not pretend the journey is easy or that spiritual formation for men can be reduced to a formula or a list we can check off and keep in our back pocket. As Michael Yaconelli suggested, honest-to-God spirituality is much messier than that (*Messy Spirituality*).[1] But I am here to say that God will transform our lives if only we begin the journey with sincerity and desire.

Beyond my "small group" of close friends, I have been privileged to know and interview dozens of men from a variety of churches and denominations, all of whom are engaged in such a spiritual expedition.

A new spiritual man

A new spiritual man is emerging in America. He does not confuse faith with politics; he does not require exclusively sports-based metaphors to gain a spiritual yard or two; he is struggling hard to be authentically Christian and countercultural in the workplace; and he understands the language of servant leadership in the home. This man is less confrontational than those who seek to effect change via condemnation and acrimony because he is learning to remember that Christ teaches us to overcome evil with good. "Be imitators of God, as beloved children, and live in love, as Christ loved us and gave himself up for us, a fragrant offering and sacrifice to God" (Eph. 5:1-2).

If he is married, the new spiritual man knows that his wife is his partner, not one more subject in his domain. If anyone asks about the dynamics of power in his family, today's disciple has learned to share the truth about relationships that are grounded in the security and freedom of God's invitation to fullness.

We live as witnesses to God's amazing and redemptive love. Relationships experienced in the context of God's social economy stand as a living testimony to our salvation, and to our independence from the warped values and skewed priorities of this broken and unsatisfying world.

One day I was confronted by an angry and insecure seminary student, a young man still struggling to make faith in Christ fit neatly with the chauvinism that had defined—and still defined—much of his life experience. He poked a bony finger in my chest and demanded to know how my wife, Rebekah, and I planned to divvy up authority in our young family.

"So who's going to be wearing the pants in your family?" he asked. "Just who will be the head of your household? Or should you get your wife's permission before you answer?"

The question wasn't as difficult as he imagined. "God is the head of our home," I replied. "But now I'm curious; tell me about yours."

Joshua answered the question this way: "Now if you are unwilling to serve the LORD, choose this day whom you will serve . . . . ; but as for me and my household, we will serve the LORD" (Josh. 24:15).

Following Christ

We all know men who tend to overcomplicate their lives with self-importance, purposeless activity, and what the preacher in Ecclesiastes describes as "vexation" and "vanity." Such chasing of the wind may define any of us. "What do mortals get from all the toil and strain with which they toil under the sun? For all their days are full of pain, and their work is a vexation; even at night their minds do not rest. This also is vanity" (Eccles. 2:22-23).

Yet at its heart, the meaning of our existence here in time and space hinges on a simple equation clearly defined by Jesus. "Truly I tell you, unless you change and become like children, you will never enter the kingdom of heaven" (Matt. 18:3).

There's nothing intimidating about Christ's caution. We can relax. Rather than one more series of hoops to jump through, Christ's words serve as a clear invitation for those who are serious about faith, a gentle reminder that we need to take another look at the essential elements of the Christian life.

Following Jesus in today's world is challenging enough without inventing new lists of do's and don'ts to feel pressured and guilty about.

What we certainly do *not* need is one more system we can flunk. What we do need is clarity of purpose, encouragement, and hope.

Jesus often pointed out that children possess qualities we would do well to emulate, especially if we want to grow spiritually. That, my friends, is good news, especially for men. As a gender we are fairly uncomplicated. Jesus speaks our language.

Why would I want to be like a child?

For starters, Jesus was all about simplicity and humility. God created us and knows how to communicate with men. Because the Creator conceived of, designed, and made us, he understands the essential simplicity and clarity of focus that characterize a man's heart.

God wants us to be like children because kids represent the kind of attitude we need to adopt if we intend to get serious about our spiritual lives.

- Youngsters are inquisitive;
- they have open minds;
- they are honest and forthright;
- they are seldom distracted by material possessions;
- they're certainly not stuck on themselves;
- they learn best by doing;
- their faith is unshakable;
- and they're not afraid of emotion.

God wants us to approach him with exactly that kind of open, child-like spirit.

Jesus was a guy: uncomplicated and direct

When God chose to come to earth in human form, he decided to make the journey as a man. That's great news! You see, God understands us. Indeed, God tailored his initial discipleship program with men in mind—flaws and all. Like us, Jesus was fairly uncomplicated, and it is no coincidence that the Gospels tell us repeatedly how children were naturally drawn to the Savior. Christ's way is the best model we have for what God has in mind for living out our faith as Christian men in a world that has lost its focus.

People always knew where they stood with Jesus; he lived honestly and with candor. The Master was truthful, disarmingly frank, and worked to make God's message clear. Here are just a few examples of the plain language Jesus typically used to express the truth about God and about how we should live as his disciples:

- No servant can serve two masters. (Luke 16:13, NIV)
- Can any of you by worrying add a single hour to your span of life? (Luke 12:25)
- I came to bring fire to the earth, and how I wish it were already kindled! (Luke 12:49)
- If your right eye causes you to sin, tear it out and throw it away. (Matt. 5:29)
- I say to you, Love your enemies and pray for those who persecute you. (Matt. 5:44)
- When you are praying, do not heap up empty phrases. (Matt. 6:7)
- Where your treasure is, there your heart will be also. (Matt. 6:21)
- Do not worry about tomorrow, for tomorrow will bring worries of its own. Today's trouble is enough for today. (Matt. 6:34)
- It is easier for a camel to go through the eye of a needle than for someone who is rich to enter the kingdom of God. (Matt. 19:24)
- Those who try to make their life secure will lose it, but those who lose their life will keep it. (Luke 17:33)
- Whoever does not carry the cross and follow me cannot be my disciple. (Luke 14:27)
- You cannot serve God and wealth. (Luke 16:13)
- After this, Jesus went out and saw a tax collector by the name of Levi sitting at his tax booth. "Follow me," Jesus said to him. (Luke 5:27, NIV)

Cut to the chase

Jesus didn't waste time. He always cut to the heart of what is important: "Follow me." He even simplified the Ten Commandments. Originally, God had delivered the essence of the law to Moses. The ten rules etched in stone served as a straightforward set of regulations. But not for long! The children of Israel got to work, probably with the help of a tentful of lawyers and a few government bureaucrats. They quickly expanded those Ten Commandments to literally thousands of complex laws and prohibitions. They turned God's loving guidance into a system of red tape that effectively trapped the religious culture in a web of legalism and perpetual disappointment.

Jesus, however, didn't mess around. He brilliantly and incisively reduced God's law to its simplest and most elegant elements.

> "You shall love the Lord your God with all your heart, and with all your soul, and with all your mind." This is the greatest and first commandment. And a second is like it: "You shall love your neighbor as yourself." On these two commandments hang all the law and the prophets. (Matt. 22:37-40)

Jesus, you see, was a man; Jesus showed us clearly how to live. And that's especially good news for men today.

I want to know God that way

We live in a world where convictions are held too loosely, where people quickly retreat into moral confusion, and where political correctness can easily suffocate creative thought.

Consequently, referring to Jesus as "100-percent man" might be considered controversial and dismissed as inappropriate in politically correct company. To be honest, I'm not sure that God cares two hoots. We cannot deny that when God chose to take on human flesh, he came to earth as a man. That fact adds up to exceptionally good news, because it means that God knows and understands me—as a man. God knows me from the inside out.

I've got to tell you, I want to know God that way. I want to know God man-to-man. I want to know that kind of Jesus. This is the context in which I am striving to live a spiritual life, and the context in which I want to understand what it means to be a Christian. Not just a Christian, but a real Christian man.

"Follow me," Jesus said. I plan to do just that.

2   A ROUND DOZEN FLAT-OUT GUYS

As Jesus passed along the Sea of Galilee, he saw Simon and his brother Andrew casting a net into the sea—for they were fishermen. And Jesus said to them, "Follow me and I will make you fish for people." And immediately they left their nets and followed him.

—*Mark 1:16-18*

It didn't take a lot of fancy schemes and tricky machinations for Jesus to secure the attention of those first followers. They were men, after all.

—Get Real, *page 26*

The first group of disciples—called by the Master himself—comprised a round dozen flat-out guys. So Jesus communicated with them accordingly.

Jesus reaches out with a simple invitation

I don't intend to disrespect Peter & Company, but the New Testament records a significant number of instances where these men came across dumber than a pile of rocks. Women love that characteristic of the disciples, and they like to point it out all the time.

So let's be clear about one fact: guys are every bit as smart as women. It's just that often we can be—well—sort of emotionally backward. We also tend to miss obvious social cues. To be frank, we need a little coaching sometimes, and that's especially true when we gather in large groups.

The disciples, the Bible tells us, simply didn't get what Jesus was all about at first.

- Then Jesus said to them, "Don't you understand this parable? How then will you understand any parable?" (Mark 4:13, NIV)

- When many of his disciples heard [Jesus], they said, "This teaching is difficult; who can accept it?" (John 6:60)
- Jesus used this figure of speech, but they did not understand what he was telling them. (John 10:6, NIV)
- Jesus answered . . . "How much longer must I put up with you?" (Matt. 17:17)
- Then Jesus' disciples said, "Now you are speaking clearly and without figures of speech." (John 16:29, NIV)

Fortunately for his new friends, and absolutely appropriate for twenty-first-century men, Jesus was the original master of the sound bite, so misunderstanding him was pretty much impossible. Jesus used short, declarative sentences such as, "Come, and you will see"; "From now on I'm going to have to call you Rocky" (author's paraphrase); "You are my friends if you do what I command you"; and "Follow me."

Not only direct but genuine

The message of Jesus was and still is alive, and his meaning unswervingly direct. Jesus didn't waste time beating around the bush. The Savior of the world always spoke the truth; indeed, genuineness was his calling card.

Jesus was all about keeping it real. He usually went—unnervingly— directly to the heart of the matter. Jesus didn't waste much time with preliminaries; he got right down to business. Yet no matter how hard he rubbed people the wrong way and how much he avoided sugarcoating his message, Jesus always treated people with the utmost respect.

Fact is, it didn't take a lot of fancy schemes and tricky machinations for Jesus to secure the attention of those first followers. They were men, after all. Jesus looked them in the eye and told them the truth. He met them, each man, at the point where their personal experience and his intention for their lives ran together in the blessed confluence of providence.

Providence is a crossroads of sorts—that compelling place where God's will and our choosing him work together. "Take heart, you would not seek me," seventeenth-century mathematician and theologian Blaise Pascal wrote, "if you had not already found me."[1]

Our great opportunity is to seize moments like that, to take Jesus at his word and to step unhesitatingly into the challenge of doing God's will. When we do, there is no telling where he might lead us. You can't put something like that on a list.

Men of providence follow without hesitation

At the beginning of John's Gospel, Jesus ran into a man called Nathanael, one of Philip's friends and probably another fisherman. Nathanael was inquisitive and evidently an honest seeker of the truth. He was curious because Jesus had made an insightful observation about his character. "When Jesus saw Nathanael approaching, he said of him, 'Here is a true Israelite, in whom there is nothing false'" (John 1:47, NIV). What Jesus said was so completely on the mark that Nathanael wanted to understand, "How is it possible this traveling teacher knows me so well?"

So Jesus told him, "'I saw you under the fig tree before Philip called you.' Nathanael replied, 'Rabbi, you are the Son of God! You are the King of Israel!'" (John 1:48-49).

Nathanael was an easy study for Jesus. The man wasn't that hard to figure out. *Holy smokes,* Nathanael must have been thinking. *How did you do that?* And just like that, another man decided to follow Christ.

We are all called to be spiritual men

Nathanael might have been a pushover to impress, but that does not mean he was shallow or unintelligent. Nathanael's response to his encounter with Christ's discerning spirit indicated that he was an uncomplicated man who nevertheless ran deep. We're not all called to be spiritual giants. We are all, however, called to be spiritual men. "Blessed are the pure in heart, for they will see God" (Matt. 5:8).

The communist philosopher Karl Marx famously dismissed religion as "the opium of the people." Faith is something, he reasoned, designed to dull our senses to the disappointing and oppressive reality of a meaningless existence. Marx contended that faith makes people easier to manage, that religion is a tool of oppression, and that God is nothing more than a made-up pawn of the ruling class.

The truth about faith in God is quite the opposite. Rather than distracting us from reality, faith is reality. Wanting to connect with the living God is a natural aspiration because our original design specifically prepared us for relationship with our Creator. Indeed, rather than keeping us docile in our society, faith in Christ should make us much more difficult to manage.

- Faith in Christ requires us to be countercultural.
- Faith in Christ is revolutionary.
- Faith seldom advocates for the status quo.
- Faith sets us free.

I'm Christian because I'm American—right?

We have a huge problem to overcome as Christian men in North America.

Somehow the phrase "Christian nation" has attained the cachet of a *fait accompli*. The definitions of *American* and of *Christian* have become so interchangeable in our culture that we're often confused about where one ends and the other begins. Even if it were true that our national roots are exclusively Christian, cultural norms have shifted a long way from the message and example of Jesus. Instead of Christ shaping who we are as American men, many people today modify their Christianity to accommodate the North American culture.

When I became a naturalized U.S. citizen back in 1985, I was thrilled to adopt a new flag, a new passport, a new constitution, and a new identity in the international community. I have memorized the Pledge of Allegiance; I get teary-eyed singing the national anthem; I root for U.S. athletes in the Olympic Games; and I have never missed an opportunity to vote. Indeed, even though my old passport still was valid in the United Kingdom (the UK recognizes dual citizenship), I decided to file away the document. I am an American citizen, period, when I travel to England or anywhere else.

But being an American, however wonderful, is not the same as being a Christian. My identity as an American is distinct from my personal faith in Christ. Despite a lot of noise from the religious right and ongoing efforts to wrap Christianity in the American flag, the two commitments are not interchangeable and never have been. Believe it or not, someone can be a great American without being a Christian, and disagreeing with my president certainly does not mean that I have turned away from God.

Some of us here in the land of plenty even buy into the idea that

God's generosity can be leveraged to reward our faith with "prosperity" as defined by our consumer culture. Mansions, luxury automobiles, fine clothes, easy-to-find parking spaces, better jobs, first-class airplane tickets, and financial freedom are touted as sure evidences of God's blessing. Many sermons market the American dream as part of the Christian life. The message is clear: Christianity looks just like middle-class America; God wants us all to be prosperous; and if we don't resemble prosperous Americans, then likely God is not blessing us.

So what does it mean to be a Christian man nowadays?

One of the great clichés of modern Christianity is WWJD (What would Jesus do?). WWJD turns out to be the wrong question. We know what Jesus would do; but I'm not Jesus, and neither are you. A better question is, "What would Jesus have *me* do?" Jesus said, "If any want to become my followers, let them deny themselves and take up their cross daily and follow me" (Luke 9:23).

The purpose of this book is to discuss how.

I have asked hundreds of people how they would answer the challenge of living as a Christian man in this culture. Dean, a Lutheran pastor friend, said the answer is pretty clearly outlined in scripture. "You want to know what it means to be a Christian man?" he asked. "Look at Philippians 2."

Paul wrote, "Do nothing from selfish ambition or conceit, but in humility regard others as better than yourselves. Let each of you look not to your own interests, but to the interests of others. Let the same mind be in you that was in Christ Jesus, who, though he was in the form of God, did not regard equality with God as something to be exploited, but emptied himself" (Phil. 2:3-7).

Following Jesus

I asked the guys in my small group to tell about a time when they felt the most connected to God, a recent experience when their faith felt vital and alive. Before the first man spoke, I said this: "I believe I know exactly what you are going to say. I'm going to write one word on a piece of paper and turn it upside down. When we're finished I'll turn it over. I can guarantee the word I have written will cover 90 percent or more of what you share."

So I spelled out my word in large letters and turned the piece of paper facedown.

Darrell volunteered first. "I guess it would have to be when we were over at the Crenshaws' house helping them out," he said. "That's the closest I've felt to God in a long time."

Jerry talked about a time he accompanied the pastor to serve Communion to people confined at home. For Eric it was taking bread to first-time visitors after church. Dave experienced grace beyond his wildest dreams as a chaperone when our youth worked with desperate people in Appalachia. Henry found God's presence during a long day on his knees cleaning the church.

And so it went around the room. Man after man sharing powerful testimonies of grace, stories of time and resources dedicated to other people's needs. Ministry in the name of Jesus Christ.

As the meeting drew to a close, I turned over my sheet of paper. I had written a single word, *SERVICE,* in bold letters.

It's not about us

It's tempting to describe spiritual formation in terms we can easily master or regulate, like a checklist or a huddle or listening to a series of teaching tapes. Such schemes can too readily become perfunctory, another sort of legalism, a way to avoid exploration and mystery, or little more than formulaic.

Being a Christian is not about us; it's about Jesus. Spiritual formation is about the life of Jesus being made visible in our bodies; it's about engaging the Spirit because we are hungry for God; it's about becoming disciples so that Jesus can pour his life into us. It's about learning to love God with our heart, mind, body, and soul. It's about having the courage to actually follow Christ—to place one foot in front of the other, to dare to live a life of grace.

Paul summed it up well: "I am confident of this, that the one who began a good work among you will bring it to completion by the day of Jesus Christ" (Phil. 1:6).

DESIRE

3 WHERE'S OUR TREASURE?

Where your treasure is, there your heart will be also.

—*Matthew 6:21*

If you indeed cry out for insight,
    and raise your voice for understanding;
if you seek it like silver,
    and search for it as for hidden treasures—
then you will understand the fear of the LORD
    and find the knowledge of God.

—*Proverbs 2:3-5*

I want to know Christ and the power of his resurrection.

—*Philippians 3:10*

A lot of people imagine that just because I write about faith, interview preachers for the newspaper, and talk a lot about Jesus, I have my spiritual stuff together. You know, gurulike and Billy Graham–esque. Fact is, at the best of times I feel like a poor student at the beginning of a long semester. I have so much to learn and a long way to go.

I'm a fellow traveler on this particular journey, so I'm as interested in where this book is going as most of you reading along. More so, probably, because I'm nothing if not a "to teach is to learn" kind of guy.

Anyway, I know and have known a lot of folk way farther down the road to having their stuff together than I, and the lessons that come from their spiritual lives give me both direction and hope. "F. W." was one such man. F. W. was deeply spiritual and loved God with all his heart, but he constantly ran hard against the management model he had mastered so thoroughly in the business world. One morning he came out of church shaking his head. "That was a powerful sermon," he said. "God really spoke to me. I must say I'm surprised."

F. W. looked legitimately puzzled, but I felt confident in picking at him because I had observed his behavior before worship. "I noticed that you came into church fifteen minutes early," I said.

"That's right," he answered.

"What were you doing all that time?" I asked. I already had a fairly good idea. "I didn't see you chatting with other people."

"Of course not," F. W. said. "That's not what that time is for. I wanted to begin worship in an attitude of prayer. I asked God to bless our time together. I prayed that God's presence would fill the sanctuary. And I asked God to speak his truth through the message."

I smiled. "Yet still you tell me that you were taken aback that God actually came through. I'm not surprised at all, F. W. Your spirit was hungry; you approached God in a manner that shouted loud and clear, 'Spirit of the living God, fall afresh on me.'[1] God delivered."

F. W.'s mind may have been loaded with evaluative questions concerning the pastor, the choice of words, the perceived fluency of delivery, the tunefulness of the choir, the particular way in which the Bible was read, or a host of other potential vexations he could possibly conjure up. But my friend had a heart for God that was open and hungry for blessing.

God honors that kind of intention. God responds to genuine desire.

Desire drives the engine

The Bible tags desire as a potent force—powerful, yes, but dangerous too. Desire crops up throughout the biblical narrative and is often associated with a move toward God. Because of its clout, however, desire is also implicated in poor decisions that cause people to fall away from God's love and grace.

We all know that desire drives people to do things they never would have imagined unless that kind of fervor had played a role. Crimes of passion are committed by people otherwise considered mild-mannered, law-abiding, or incapable of such deeds. Likewise, the desire to achieve, to serve, or to know God has provided the drive behind many extraordinary accomplishments.

While passion is often considered an explanation for antisocial behavior, it is not a valid excuse. Desire can be harnessed, doused, indulged, or set aside; it's entirely our choice. The apostle Paul makes the point many times that even though desire is a potent force, our passions certainly fall within the parameters of self-control.

While desire is implicated in a boatload of sins (the Bible refers to evil desires, human desires, sinful desires, corrupt desires, lustful desires, deceitful desires, harmful desires, etc.), the scriptures also point to desire as perhaps the key ingredient, or catalyst, to spiritual growth.

> As a deer longs for flowing streams,
>   so my soul longs for you, O God.
> My soul thirsts for God,
>   for the living God.
> When shall I come and behold
>   the face of God?
> My tears have been my food
>   day and night,
> while people say to me continually,
>   "Where is your God?" (Ps. 42:1-3)

Ask any marketing guru

Jesus said it many times and in many ways. "Where your treasure is, there your heart will be also" (Matt. 6:21). Snag a man's desire, and you will pretty much have all of his attention.

I'm a guy. I like cars. Guys like car commercials. Manufacturers put car commercials on all the time during sports shows because they know how easily we salivate at the pop of a hood. They don't even need to drape the cars with girls. Testosterone can be measured in horsepower, and we're suckers, every one of us.

One of my favorite examples of manipulation is a commercial that features a vehicle fully loaded with several cool options nobody really needs. Fun to look at, but obviously out of my price range. However, just when I'm ready to dismiss the product, a smooth-toned voice-over sows just the faintest seed of doubt in my mind by saying, "Not luxury you don't need, just luxury you're not used to."

Advertising works because people will do just about anything to fulfill their desires. If we can convince ourselves that what we desire is also something we need, then they just about have us—hook, line, and sinker. Once we set our hearts on something, we tend to move heaven and earth. Think about it; why else would an otherwise sane man go four thousand dollars in debt for a 60-inch plasma television when he already has a 24-inch set that works perfectly well?

Before we know it, the entire focus of our lives can become the acquisition of more and more possessions. Control the desire, and we can begin to control the rest of our lives.

Yes, it's that simple.

Freedom and desire

Ask any man what distinguishes him from a prisoner or a citizen of a nation controlled by a totalitarian regime, and he will answer, "I have the freedom to make my own choices. I can travel where and when I want to. I can pursue any career I please. I can make my own decisions about how I use my time and how I allocate my resources. I call the shots."

Oh really? Is that so? It turns out that we give up that kind of freedom on a daily basis. We sell our birthright for the proverbial bowl of stew (Gen. 24:19-34) with very little resistance.

- We feel compelled to buy stuff we don't need, seldom use, and rarely enjoy.
- We say we don't have time for family because we're working overtime to pay for all those things we were told we need to make us happy.
- We drink too much, smoke cigarettes, or hang out at bars because the people on the commercials looked happy when they were doing that.
- We neglect our spiritual life because "Guys don't do that kind of thing. Men would rather watch sports on TV, drink beer, and isolate themselves from substantive relationships." Meanwhile we're dying inside, and our souls are drying up from neglect.

If we are indeed the free agents we insist we are, then can we explain why we so obediently chase after every material carrot dangled in front of our faces by our consumer culture, and why our desires follow the advertising budgets of the people who work so hard to manipulate us?

When that happens—when we have lost our freedom and our ability to discriminate— Jesus said we can't even hear his words anymore. "The cares of the world, and the lure of wealth, and the desire for other things come in and choke the word, and it yields nothing" (Mark 4:19).

This is not a new predicament

Good news! We're not the first. The children of Israel ran into the same kinds of problems when it came to making their own choices. They let their desires become directed and influenced by the ambient culture instead of being instructed by the living God. They thought that what they wanted was a king. They didn't really know why, or even what good it would do; they simply knew that everyone else had one and that was enough.

God said, "That's not the kind of society I had in mind for you." But his people insisted. Please, please, please, pretty please, God. Just give us this, and we won't ask for anything else. "We want a king over us. Then we will be like all the other nations" (1 Sam. 8:19-20, NIV).

Haven't we all heard the same conversation at home?

- "Other parents let their kids have a TV in their room."
- "The other kids at school watch R-rated movies."
- "All my friends do it!"
- "I *know* we can't afford a pool, but so many of our neighbors have one."
- "Both my partners at work drive a Hummer."
- "All the other attorneys joined the country club."
- "No one else needs God to make it through life."
- "I don't need the study group; besides, all the other guys are watching the game."
- "Why can't we be just like all the other nations?"

Maybe I'm missing something here. Just what is so appealing about being just like all the other nations, all the other neighbors, or all the other guys? Why should we fall for the same false desires that trap everyone else? For crying out loud! As Christians aren't we supposed to be a little different?

A lie, repeated often enough . . . is still a lie

So what are we told? What do we listen to, every day and a thousand times a day, in and via absolutely every form of media? What message are we receiving? What does the world, the ambient culture, tell us we are supposed to desire?

- Sex. Not just sex but sex without commitment.
- Youth. Age is the enemy. We are coached to desire products that mask or slow down the physical evidence of aging.
- Cars. Fast, powerful, expensive. (You know you want it!)
- Larger, more luxurious homes.
- Cutting-edge technology.
- The *appearance* of contentment. Note the word *appearance*.

The fork in the road: Why do we listen?

So why do we allow ourselves to be hoodwinked? That's a good question to think about. Why do we continue to vigorously seek after lifestyle-defining trinkets that have failed to satisfy, do fail to satisfy, and undoubtedly will fail to satisfy in the future?

It's as if we have created such a huge lie that we feel compelled to work even harder to justify the deception, the deeper in we find ourselves.

In a bizarre twist, many Americans have even fine-tuned their religion to accommodate such thinking. Eternal truths recast to equate spiritual blessing with material gain. Rather than realigning our values to match the genuineness of such messages as Christ's Sermon on the Mount, the image of Jesus is tweaked and finessed to the extent that some preachers now voice-over the Savior, saying, "Blessed are the well-to-do, for they have received the favor of God."

Sometimes I almost detect a sense of desperation in America. It has to be true, we cry; our consumer culture has to be the answer to the meaning of life, or why would we have sold our souls so readily?

I'm talking about freedom here. Freedom to choose our passion and the freedom to nurture our desire. If we take back our desire, the rest of the journey will fall into place with less distraction. Until that time, we have a fight on our hands every time we come to a fork in the road, and only one of the alternative paths leads to spiritual maturity.

But I guarantee this: *We will follow our desire.*

God honors our desire to grow spiritually

One of my favorite Bible stories is all about spiritual desire, compounded by time and obedience. Longing mixed with patience—and that's not an easy combination for men! The characters are elderly, their names Simeon and Anna, and you can read all about them in Luke 2:25-38, just after the Christmas story.

> Now there was a man in Jerusalem whose name was Simeon; this man was righteous and devout, looking forward to the consolation of Israel, and the Holy Spirit rested on him. . . .
>
>   There was also a prophet, Anna. . . . She was of a great age, . . . a widow to the age of eighty-four. She never left the temple but worshiped there with fasting and prayer night and day. (vv. 25, 36-37)

Simeon and Anna were two people who loved God; they owned a deep desire to know God more completely. They had the "want-to," and it multiplied over a long, long time. They both earnestly desired a personal revelation of God's love, and they were among the first in Israel to bear witness to the infant Jesus.

Here is the beautiful part. Anna and Simeon might have had to wait until they were old (it's quite possible they had held on to the promises since they were young people), but the spiritual growth they experienced, over time and in response to their desire, left them well prepared to receive God's revelation when the time came. Genuine desire, you see, hangs in for the long haul. Simeon went on to say this:

> Master, now you are dismissing
>   your servant in peace,
>   according to your word;
> for my eyes have seen your salvation. (Luke 2:29-30)

Baby steps to spiritual desire

My friend Roger became a spiritual giant in my eyes the other day. I believe it was the combination of honesty, dogged belief, and the compelling spirit of authenticity with which he told his story.

"I wanted to say no when the pastor asked me to share today," he said. "But what came out of my mouth was yes.

"Yes was the correct response," he smiled, "because then I knew I had to listen to God."

Roger's desire came along as secondary to his obedience. Yet it was desire just the same. As he prepared to talk about the ways God had worked in his life in the past, something spiritual and immediate took place—Roger noticed that God actually was working in his life, not just in the past but also in the present moment.

Because Roger desired to have a story to tell, God graciously gave him one. Or, rather, God revealed afresh to my friend the story he had been experiencing all along. Sometimes it's simply a matter of paying attention.

"When I tried to remember some specific moment in my faith journey," Roger said, "all that came to my mind was the image of a dark night. So was God telling me nothing? I thought so at first, but then I realized that was not the truth at all; because as I stared into the darkness trying to listen, one by one, tiny pinpricks of light began to appear."

As Roger was speaking I couldn't help but remember our great trek out west several years ago. We embarked on a three-week family vacation to New Mexico, Arizona, Utah, and Colorado. The children were going on seventh and ninth grades, and we drove more than eight thousand miles. Once in a while we experienced some rough spots in family communication. OK, I'll be a little more honest: a few days around the beginning of Utah were absolute hell.

One such day found us in Bryce Canyon National Park. My wife, Rebekah, and I talked about the negative spiral, asked God for guidance, and then decided to choose unconditional love wrapped in unbounded grace. We took the children to the park lodge for a first-class meal, gave them both a generous gift, and had a marvelous time together. After supper we drove through the twilight to the far southeast of the park, a remote outlook known as Bryce Point. We pulled out the sleeping bags and laid them on a grassy knoll.

"We don't leave this place until everyone sees a shooting star," Rebekah said. The children grumbled a little, but they lay down and peered into the growing darkness.

"Nothing's there," Naomi said. "They must not have stars in Utah."

We smiled but held our tongues.

"I think I can see Venus," Andrew chimed in after a few minutes, adding a brief lecture on the difference between planets and stars.

Something wonderful happens when you pause, catch your breath, and look searchingly into the clear night sky. Every few seconds a new light pops into focus, and every minute or so a deeper layer of space is revealed. Planets, satellites, constellations, nebulae, and our own galaxy—the fine mist of the Milky Way.

By the time I saw my fourth—or was it fifth?—shooting star (the one that nicely dissected the Big Dipper), the night sky was a riot of light and color. God's revealing evidence had been there all along. We simply had to have the patience—and the desire—to look.

And so at church that night my friend Roger began to identify a few pinpricks of light he began to see emerging from his ongoing journey of faith. He soon realized, he said, that he had been blessed immeasurably with the evidence of so much grace in his life.

Then—and here's where his testimony resonated so purely with my spirit—he said that in the act of watching all of those stars come out, in the discipline of remembering, his desire to know God more was rekindled. The blazing radiance of God's glory had just begun to truly be revealed to him.

The longer and the more expectantly we look into a night sky, the more stars emerge, bright pinpricks of grace and devotion. Roger found that by searching his own heart, by the very wanting, little by little the darkness lit up until the firmament of his spirit shone bright with the dazzling truth. "And the Word became flesh and lived among us, and we have seen his glory, the glory as of a father's only son, full of grace and truth" (John 1:14).

4 SETTING OUR MINDS ON THE THINGS OF THE SPIRIT

Those who live according to the flesh set their minds on the things of the flesh, but those who live according to the Spirit set their minds on the things of the Spirit.

—*Romans 8:5*

Polite conversation before and after funerals tends to be quiet and somewhat superficial. You know, the "low, respectful buzz," or surface mode of exchange. Certain protocols need to be observed. Indeed, outside of the reception line where both hugs and words are heartfelt and sincere, most dialogue tends to be safely limited to pleasantry, particularly among strangers.

I attended a memorial service recently where the memories, the stories, and the scriptures touched everyone deeply. The celebration was both heartfelt and poignant, and there were more tears of joy and gratitude than bitterness or gloom. Everyone present was uplifted and inspired, and the entire congregation enjoyed the opportunity to reflect on the remembrance of a life well lived.

Later, mourner after mourner stood and told stories about how this man had touched their lives. Some shared memories that most of us already knew; some gave more intimate glimpses; some read from a prepared page; some folk gushed from the heart until they simply ran out of things to say; and some merely stood in front of the podium and cried unashamedly.

In the lobby after the service, munching hors d'oeuvres and sipping punch, I found myself in conversation with a man who was unfamiliar with positive funerals.

"What a wonderful service," he exclaimed. "I was deeply moved. When I die," the man continued, "I want that pastor to do my funeral."

He took another bite of an egg salad sandwich and chased it with a swig of punch. "In fact," he said earnestly, "I want the service to be just like this one—the same music, the same Bible readings, the same words."

I smiled. Our church doesn't do cookie-cutter or fill-in-the-blank funeral services. Everything that was shared, said, read, or sung pertained specifically to the loving life of generosity and Christian service that "Timothy" had lived.

My response caught both of us off guard (see paragraph one on the previous page, regarding funeral small-talk protocol). "If you want to have a funeral like this one," I said, looking him directly in the eye, "then you are going to have to live a life like Timothy's between now and when you die."

In his classic book *The 7 Habits of Highly Effective People,* author Stephen Covey begins by asking readers to imagine a series of friends standing up to speak at a memorial when their life is over. The stories we would like them to tell, Covey suggests, and the achievements we would want to see referenced, amount to a good starting place when we consider our long-term goals.[1]

It doesn't matter if we are twelve, thirty-five, sixty-eight, or pushing ninety, each one of us has the privilege and the opportunity to engage the time we have available with the conscious application of meaning and purpose.

The man I was talking with was blown away by the sense of purpose and completion evidenced in the life of the deceased. He was deeply impressed by the genuine meaning vested in a life so graciously lived. He wanted his life to resonate with the same kind of significance.

Fortunately, what he wanted so badly was not outside the realm of possibility, and it is a fairly simple goal to achieve for any one of us. But he was 100 percent wrong in believing it had anything to do with the minister preaching the funeral. It has everything to do with desire, with focused aspiration, and with our willingness to satisfy that hunger by deciding to follow Jesus.

My new friend now has the opportunity to choose to live the life of abundance and deliberate service God specifically designed him to experience. He has the opportunity to turn ordinary into extraordinary by following Christ. It is no accident that the memorial service touched him so profoundly—because the substance of the life that was eulogized that day spoke to a deep place inside him where truth resides.

For me, three distinct certainties emerged from our conversation:

1. Each moment holds the possibility of fullness; that is our opportunity.
2. Each day can be a gift we share with a needy world; that is our decision.
3. Each lifetime bears the fruit of those daily decisions; that will be our legacy.

The man walked out of the church with desire brimming over in his heart, mind, and soul. Because of that, anything at all is possible.

Testimony

At my church, Wednesday evenings rock. Each week during worship someone from the congregation stands up to share a short anecdote from his or her life, something that illustrates an experience of faith or a moment of grace. The stories have been so remarkable in their simplicity and clarity that I have learned to arrive at church with a sense of anticipation: "What are you planning to teach me today, Lord?"

My friend David is an airline pilot. He has the skill to land a 737 pretty much anywhere and the confidence to back it up. David is all about discipline and self-control. In his story he shared about his family and a stressful time when he was forced to completely rely on faith. The experience helped him realize how much God means to him, and now he is even more hungry for God.

John is an intellectual. He has advanced degrees and loves to read. He can argue circles around anyone on just about any subject. He's also an outdoorsman, rugged and self-reliant. He recounted a time the Holy Spirit touched him so deeply that he simply broke down and cried. "Not very 'manly,'" he smiled, "and not something you can wrap your mind around intellectually. God taught me so much that day."

You read Roger's story at the end of the last chapter. Once he owned his desire to know God and made a point of asking God to teach him, his spiritual journey began to take on new definition and meaning. I have heard this theme repeated on countless occasions—God's gracious response when we present him with humble, receptive hearts.

Desire as a prelude to experience

I often wonder what I will say when it is my turn to share. I have loved God for many years, and in thinking about my personal history, I realize there is much I could draw on, some great stories of God working in my family and through my life. But the other morning, driving along a country road on my way to interview a local character for the newspaper, I felt an acute sense of spiritual desire. I wanted to know God more completely, and I wanted to understand a moment of grace right then, on that particular day.

Not previously, but right now. I wanted immediacy, because sometimes the memory of belief is not enough.

In a flash of insight—unusual for me on a weekday before noon—I knew I had stumbled across a potentially life-shaping moment. I realized I should pay close attention. I understood with great clarity that what I really want, more than anything, is an up-to-the-minute testimony to share; something fresh and compelling that's brand-new every day; a spiritual journey that's constantly moving forward and upward. My old stories are fine, and I pray that I always remember them, but God's love is new every morning. Not just now but this afternoon, not just today but tomorrow, not just this week but next week too.

I have this desire, and that morning I felt it more deeply than ever.

I want a spiritual life that is always on the move. I want my definition of what it means to be a Christian man to constantly expand. If someone asks me to say anything about what God has been up to in my life, I want to be able to talk about today.

"God," I said, firmly keeping both hands on the wheel and vaguely anticipating some kind of a sign. "I want to know you more."

Nothing happened. To be honest, it was just as I expected, the way I always talk with God—just the blur of traffic and the constant sound of the radio chattering.

I persisted nonetheless. "God, I'm trying to be honest with you here." I felt a little desperate now. "I'd kind of appreciate something in the way of a spiritual experience that I can talk about in church. I really do want to know you more."

"No, you don't!"

I felt the truth of the words pressing in on me, soundless yet clear, transferred into my consciousness with precision and resonance.

Unmistakably recognizable as my Lord, like picking out the cry of your own child on a crowded playground. It was as close to an audible voice as I could experience.

"What do you mean?" I ventured. The underlying tone of cosmic cynicism was not what I had expected.

I could almost hear God sigh. *"I mean exactly what you heard. 'No— you—do—not!' You really don't want to know me more. Understand?"*

This time I couldn't even speak. I just thought, or felt rather, a sense of wanting God to spell it out for me while simultaneously realizing he was already doing just that. I also understood that such unambiguous communication is rare; maybe what I needed to do was to pay attention.

"Right now you're listening to mean-spirited talk radio. Before that it was some clown on a so-called morning show. You're thinking about your interview. You're scrolling through messages on your cell phone. You're trying to decide whether to pass the slow car in front of you. You're so distracted I couldn't get your attention if I tried! You asked, so now you know. Your move."

I was suddenly sure, in that moment, that I honestly did want to know God more. I knew it with a sense of anticipation and assurance, even though I had been acting all along as if my spiritual life was little more than an afterthought.

I felt intense desire for God bubbling up from inside me. It was undeniably real. So I turned off the radio, stashed my cell phone, opened the windows, pulled back the moon roof (God had laid on a beautiful day), and loaded a Christian music CD into the car stereo. The words hit hard, as if they were penned just for me:

> No more, my God, I boast no more
> Of all the duties I have done;
> I quit the hopes I held before,
> To trust the merits of thy Son.[2]

I drove within my limits, content to follow the speed of the vehicles ahead, and I let the lyrics settle into my spirit. I paid attention to God.

"No more": no more distractions. "No more, my God": know God more. No more garbage saturating my brain. Know my God. No more simply fitting in my spiritual life, choosing times and places where God is merely a convenience. "No more, my God." No more. I really do want to know you.

I pulled over. I had to. I needed to concentrate completely on my intention to know. I needed to capitalize on my desire. It wasn't enough to be convicted. It wasn't even enough to feel blessed. I had to follow up.

And it wasn't hard, not that particular step. It wasn't even that dramatic. My eyes welled up, but I didn't cry. My mouth formed words, but my prayer wasn't eloquent. My spirit soared, but I didn't experience ecstasy. My senses, though, my intention, my focus—these had all completely changed. When I got back on the road, I drove to my interview as a different kind of man.

Now there was no question but that I was a spiritual man who happened to be driving a car. I knew that the invitation to God's presence must encompass everything, even driving. Undeniably I was a Christian journalist—God would be disarmingly present during my interview. God had leaked into my active consciousness, and that made all the difference in the world.

If they asked me, I thought, I could tell the story next Wednesday night. But I'm praying that tomorrow God will teach me something new.

You can't get what you don't want

Most members of my generation are familiar with the classic Rolling Stones song "You Can't Always Get What You Want." The lyrics may indeed speak truth in the world of human relationships and romantic love. We can't always get what we want, but we might manage to get what we need if only we try hard enough. Tenacity pays off. Fair enough.

In the arena of spiritual growth, however, wanting turns out to be a fundamental prerequisite for making any progress at all. When our wanting lines up with God's intention, that combination adds up to one powerful recipe. When the heartfelt longing of Christian men is the desire to walk in God's way, look out, world! In that case, what we want is most certainly and powerfully what we are going to get.

For Christian men, wanting is absolutely the most critical variable in the equation. God will never force his hand if we fail to own the desire. Coercion is not in God's nature, and bullying is not in his game plan. The Lord of the universe has always been gracious to respect the choices we make.

The ball is in our court. "You've got to have the want-to" may be a worn cliché in religious vernacular, but it turns out to be a powerful truth. In practice a large enough dose of want-to adds up to an enormously effective tool on the infrequently traveled road of ongoing spiritual formation.

DISCIPLESHIP

5 THE STRUCTURE OF A WELL-GROUNDED FAITH

Surely I know the plans I have for you, says the LORD, plans for your welfare and not for harm, to give you a future with hope.

—Jeremiah 29:11

My friend Don Zegel plays trombone for the Florida Orchestra.

Sometimes when he sits on the stage, just one man in the middle of a mass of musicians, Don simply lets the music wash over him. "I feel this admiration and thankfulness," he said, genuinely awestruck. "It's one of the biggest thrills, just to be there."

In a well-known anecdote about his decision to become a Christ-follower, author C. S. Lewis described his conversion to Christianity as a gradual realization, one that he was able to narrow down to a particular journey on a bus. He said that when he boarded the bus he was not a Christian, but when he finally arrived at his destination he realized that he was.

If you ask Don the trombonist to pinpoint the day and the hour when he turned to Christ, he'll likely come up with something more like this: "In 1965 when I walked into my first college class, I was not a Christian. When I was recovering from my heart attack in 1999, I realized that I was."

The unexpected cardiac event certainly captured my friend's attention, but he was quick to realize that God had in effect been speaking to him for three decades. The circumstances of the precipitating event left Don not only shaken but incredulous. He wanted to argue with the doctors.

"I was saying, 'No, you're wrong!'" Don explained. "I didn't want to hear that a guy my age—who didn't eat dessert and ran twenty-five miles a week—could have a heart attack."

Surprises aren't supposed to happen to technically proficient musicians who dot all the i's and cross all the t's in their lives. Don was further insulted a couple of weeks later when new pain led to another hospital stay, and his doctors prescribed a stress test. He was scared that he would fail, and he said he wasn't ready for that much reality all at once. He knew he was losing control.

The man in the adjacent bed—another Don—was in bad shape. Yet as visitors came and went, the musician became aware that his counterpart was alive, compassionate, and more concerned for other people's lives than his own. The man was obviously devout and at peace; faith was his sure companion.

"I was in a panic that I might fail the stress test," Don said, still bemused at his own need for control. "The more I thought about it, the more nervous I became. I started to freak."

Eventually Don buzzed a nurse and asked for medicine to help him relax. Her response was priceless. "I'll bring you your Xanax," she promised, "but drugs or no drugs, we need to talk. If you take that Xanax without talking to me, you're going to fall asleep—but everything you need to talk about is still going to be in there."

So Don the trombone player poured it all out. The worries, the fears, the injustice of it all; his need to be in control. "She was an angel," he said. "I really mean that. Right then and there I started to cry; I mean I started to sob. She listened and said, 'You don't live alone on this planet.'

"I was really ashamed," he continued, "because the other Don turned out to be concerned about me. A week later I read that he had passed away. It was obvious that his whole family had great faith. This guy was so strong and so at peace."

The experience placed everything in perspective.

"I had assumed that by this point in my life I would be principal trombonist in one of the big orchestras," Don said. "But what I have learned to realize is my purpose in relation to creation, my purpose in terms of why God gave me these particular gifts, and what he wants me to do with them."

Don had already visited church a few times as a guest musician. I don't routinely go to the hospitals, but I felt strongly led to visit him during his stay.

"I told the pastor I wasn't sure enough," he told me, "and that I didn't think I had enough faith to be a Christian. But she said if I was ready to make a commitment, then Christ was willing to meet me right where I was. Jesus didn't let me down."

Don now understands his lifelong journey more and more in the context of the language of faith. "It makes so much more sense," he said, "when it is all about God and not all about Don Zegel.

"I now realize," he continued, "that I have enough ability to do whatever I am called to do. It just hit me one day: it's not about what I want; it's about what God wants for me. That makes everything all right.

"I've learned that my job doesn't make me any more valuable than any other person, and that brings a lot of freedom. Even if I had one of these absolutely major jobs, I wouldn't be free unless I realized that the guy who helped me find the #1 screws at Home Depot was every bit as important to the workings of the world."

Like someone who always wakes up with fresh eyes, Don emanates a sense of wonder and a quiet peace. He talks about the orchestra with awe, reflects on his faith with deep gratitude, and regards his family with consummate love.

He is that grateful now, that much at peace.

It might have been the Benadryl

I had a sort of vision the other day. Of course, it might have been the Benadryl. Spring oak blossom allergies have hit me rather badly this year, so I sometimes have to lie down with a cold washcloth on my forehead and pop a couple of antihistamines.

Anyway, the vision looked a little like this. I saw a road stretching ahead, a pathway meandering over hills, through woods, and even in the middle of towns and busy cities. The path didn't look anything at all like the classically pious or religious roads we read about in books such as *The Pilgrim's Progress*. Instead of a narrow and lonely "road less traveled," this one was fairly well populated. I saw quite a number of people in my vision; some were moving forward in groups, and others walked by themselves—but everyone was going along in the same direction, and undoubtedly we were all making the journey together.

I felt clearly that I was observing the kind of spiritual pilgrimage God invites me to take—a journey in community and not just by myself.

We're in this together, you know

One of the greatest things about living in community—and by community I mean The Men's Room group and the relationships I have with my wife, my extended family, and my other friends at church—is the sense of shared story, the profound understanding that there is companionship and wisdom along the way. I believe that this sense of community has been and still is the critical component in my ongoing spiritual formation.

Eugene Peterson describes Christian discipleship as "a long obedience in the same direction."[1] I like his image very much. I'd love one day to reflect on my own experience in retrospect and observe a gradual, forward, upward-moving curve. It is one of those picture-perfect ideals. My personal truth, however, has been a series of fits and starts—both ups and downs—a journey sometimes in many directions and marked with loops; successes, retreats, and failures that dot the landscape of my faith.

My faith journey is kind of like my relationship to the guitar. You'd think I'd be a master of six strings and twenty frets by now, considering when I first set the instrument against the wall in the corner of my room—about the same time I invited Jesus to be Lord of my life.

Today, well over thirty years later, I still buzz the strings almost every time I play.

The two journeys, it occurs to me now, have been strikingly parallel.

Confident and cool

I really only wanted the guitar at first because a couple of people I admired looked so confident and cool strumming along and singing choruses after church. I learned three chords right off and was able to play along with about half a dozen songs. But I didn't bother to understand the music or even take the time to learn the names of the notes. Instead, I called the shapes I made with my fingers #1, #2, and #3. Much later I learned that those particular patterns on the fingerboard represented the chords D, A7, and G. I was not exactly racing ahead.

My guitar was an entry-level nylon-stringed "classic," and it traveled almost everywhere with me. I genuinely liked it, and even though I learned very little and played only at a rudimentary level, the instrument became a prop that helped define me—if only in the vague sense of who I thought I should be.

There have been seasons of my life when that faithful guitar has spent weeks or months forgotten in a closet somewhere, gathering dust. Sometimes I pick it up only to discover I have forgotten some rudimentary skill, that I have become extraordinarily rusty, that the strings need to be replaced, or that I have slid far backward. Once in a while I have even dusted off my instrument, played a few notes, and realized that I am not interested anymore. With a shrug I put it away and turn my attention to some other distraction.

Then there are those times I feel the stirring of music deep inside me, wild and insistent. Then I can't wait to get my instrument out and play. That's when I move forward in leaps and bounds. At times like those—full of new songs, elaborate chords, and the deep joy of discovery—I wonder why I ever let the music get away from me in the first place.

It was during one of those musical seasons that I first met my wife, and the early part of our falling in love involved a lot of guitar. "You play my heartstrings," she said. The first year we were married, Rebekah pulled together all of her resources and bought me the beautiful Ovation Balladeer acoustic guitar that sits behind me as I write. The guitar has a gorgeous tone, and it helped sustain my infatuation with the six-string. I wrote some great songs for her during those years and soaked up everything I could possibly learn.

But even love songs take a backseat sometimes to new lives and children and busyness and careers. Mastery is ever elusive, and not even the most powerful desire can take the place of the critical need for guidance that both my music and my faith have always required to prosper beyond the initial burn.

Committed and growing

A few years ago we started a praise band at church. In that context commitment took over where my desire has always tended to fall short. Simply put, I placed myself and my Ovation in a position of discipline and encouragement, and my ability to play has grown accordingly.

It turns out my faith is a lot like that.

Being a disciple of Jesus is much like playing guitar in the band. While desire may be the spark that ignites the fire, my spiritual journey flames out with relative ease—all too readily and distressingly quickly. My love for God can also find its way into the closet, and there it gathers dust; God does not force his presence on me any more than my neglected instrument will leap into my hands to say, "Let's play."

There's a lot to be said for showing up to play music with the band every week, for picking up my guitar every day, and for running through even the simplest songs of praise. In the middle of such routine acts of devotion, I often find that God's love sneaks up on me unawares.

It's that "long obedience in the same direction" idea again.

It's all about intention

My wife and I have been married for twenty-seven years. Our life together continues to be a wonderful journey, but we have also learned how important it is to rely on something more consistent than passion and desire if we want to move the relationship forward.

Here's my secret: it's all about intention. My decision to love Rebekah is more reliable than the hot and cold changeability of romance—however much fun that portion of our marriage continues to be. I begin every single day of our life together—not just weekends or just when I feel like it—by bringing her a hot mug of tea or coffee in bed and hanging around to read a few stories together from the morning newspaper.

But what if I don't particularly like her on any given day? What if we had a serious argument the night before? What if she has to get up earlier than I want to, and I happen to be extra tired that morning? What if I don't feel the slightest stirrings of love in my heart, or what if coldness and distance have developed between us?

All these challenges and difficulties have been factors over the past three decades. They are in every marriage. But rather than shrink back into my cocoon, I especially make sure to bring her a hot drink in bed on mornings like those.

The secret of tea

I essentially call all of this the secret of tea. Of course, it's really about loving well, and unmistakably it's all about playing the sweetest and the most beautiful music on my guitar, and obviously it's also very much about moving from simple desire into an intentional spiritual formation that is ongoing and true.

I grew up in England, across the other side of the Big Pond. Consequently, the residual British-tea gene is fixed as a deeply important element of my social and behavioral profile. I may drink a lot of coffee, especially when I need to prop my eyes open and write, but there is a quality to tea—and its preparation—that I believe can be instructive when we think about the dynamics of how healthy relationships progress.

Apart from antioxidant, heart fitness, and other amazing health benefits my friends in the granola crowd will likely tout, the real genius behind tea resides in its redemptive and civilizing characteristics. Tea is all about the preparation, the time invested, and the intention to drink together in community. Most important, however, the preparation and the sharing of a pot of tea is a deliberate act of grace.

Let me explain. The teapot is my favorite gift to give as a wedding present, and the instructions I sometimes enclose read a lot like this:

Please read the following before preparing tea:

- Life is inherently difficult. As beings made in the image of God, our unique design encourages us to act on our environment with creative purpose. Each challenge we face is in truth an opportunity to engage the intention of creation and to live on the cutting edge of possibility. Marriage is loaded with such opportunity. Tea can help here.
- Love is never about winning but always about healing. The best relationships nurture one another. As men, especially, our primary responsibility is to love our wives. (If you believe that the famous "submission" passage in Ephesians 5:21-33 is all about wives obeying husbands and men getting everything they want, we need to talk.) Love means nurture; nurture means service; and service means tea.
- Preparing and serving a hot cup of tea is a selfless and redemptive act of practical love. Here's how it works:

    Imagine that you are in trouble with your spouse (this works equally well if you are not, but let's deal with reality). Say, "Let's have a cup of tea." This is code for: "I want to sit down with you and serve you. I want to share some meaningful time with you."
    It takes time to boil water (the microwave does not make good tea). It takes time to properly warm the pot before pouring

the boiling water over the leaves. It takes time to let the tea steep to perfection. It takes time to pour the tea into china cups or mugs and then to select the appropriate cookie or cracker.

When you finally sit down with your spouse, you bring a good ten minutes of preparation and positive intention to a well-considered act of deliberate, loving service. Consequently, you have created the opportunity for healing dialogue.

Offering tea declares, "I love you enough to serve you; to prepare something with the entire civilizing weight of British history behind it; to spend ten minutes—knee to knee—sipping something good, making eye contact, and offering my full attention." It says, "I want this relationship to work."

I have made tea for my wife, Rebekah, as late as one o'clock in the morning. Neither one of us was looking for a hot drink, but we certainly needed the ritual.

OK. Enough with the wedding gift instructions. So what has this got to do with spiritual formation?

Everything, it turns out. Making the conscious effort to do something intentional and beneficial with a relationship is always our opportunity, irrespective of how we feel.

Making tea.

Practicing my guitar.

Committing ourselves to the discipline of daily time and attention regarding our relationship with God. What better way to grow spiritually than through the generous love of deliberate action?

Conscious effort is the first and the biggest step toward the "becoming" part of spiritual formation—the decision and the discipline of it—the element that lost its way so easily when all we had to fall back on was our desire.

In men's group "Gerry" pointed out the infrequent occurrence of the miraculous in most of our day-to-day lives. "It's not that we are looking for something spectacular in particular," he said. "But things just happen around people of great faith who choose to believe."

He is exactly right. Saying "I choose you, Jesus; it is my intention and my goal as a man to follow more deliberately in your way" can open the door to the most amazing things.

6   LEARNING TO IMPROVISE

But their delight is in the law of the LORD,
    and on his law they meditate
        day and night.
They are like trees
    planted by streams of water.

—Psalm 1:2-3

I told my musician friend Don I'd like to learn to play jazz and
blues on my guitar. He gave me a book, but 75 percent of the pages
contained nothing but scales. "But I want to improvise," I said.
"You can't improvise unless you have something to improvise
from," he answered.

—Get Real, pages 61–62

Do not think that I have come to abolish the law or the prophets;
I have come not to abolish but to fulfill. For truly I tell you, until
heaven and earth pass away, not one letter, not one stroke of a
letter, will pass from the law until all is accomplished.

—Matthew 5:17-18

What I really want to do is learn how to play blues and jazz on my
guitar. I love the way jazz musicians lay out a simple theme and then
play all around it. I'm fascinated by the virtuosity, the unbounded freedom, and by the way new ideas seem to pour out of a deep well.

I told Don, the trombone musician, about it. The next week at
rehearsal he handed me a book. "Everything you need is right here,"
he said.

So I dove in. I was devastated to find that 75 percent of the pages
contained nothing but scales. "What's up with that?" I complained. "I
want to learn the part where I can just take off and get all bluesy."

"You don't understand," he told me. "You can't improvise unless you have something to improvise from. If you don't memorize all the scales first, you'll be pulling from a dry well."

Eric is a high school science teacher. He is also a PhD biologist and one of the most intelligent men I know. Eric's journey to faith started in his midtwenties. Essentially, some other men he knew and respected made a positive witness to their faith. They owned up to feeling some excitement about their spiritual journey. More importantly, they weren't afraid to talk about it.

So Eric decided to show up at church for his son's baptism. He stood with his wife for the ceremony and then sat in the pew for the remainder of the service in a defensive posture with his arms folded. But his ears were nowhere near all the way closed, and his heart was open at least just a smidgen.

What Eric observed was a vibrant community of faith with as many men present as women. That made him curious, because it flew in the face of certain stereotypes presented to him for most of his life.

Not only were there men in the congregation, but many of these men were in their twenties, thirties, and forties. That surprised Eric because these guys could have been doing so many other things—yet there they were, worshiping God, unapologetic and full of peace.

When he talked further with the men he met at church—and he got to do that because they invited him to join them for Sunday school, and he was curious enough to come back—Eric discovered, again to his surprise, that these were intelligent, thinking men. They weren't afraid to engage him in conversation or entertain hard questions.

Today, in The Men's Room, Eric is committed to learning enough of the more basic and fundamental scales so that he can begin to improvise.

One day a couple of The Men's Room guys said they were a little jealous of Eric's newbie status. They wondered if they'd feel their faith differently if they were brand-new Christians. "You have a much more exciting story," one of them said to Eric. "Sometimes I think it would be great if my faith was fresh and new like yours."

Faith is certainly "new every morning," and the Christian life can be exhilarating every day. But my personal experience resonated with the other guys': it's all too easy to slip into a sense of sameness and routine.

Eric's reply was both astounding and profound. His answer may have been off-the-cuff, yet at the same time it was deeply insightful. Reality is always telling, and my friend's honest response reminded me of an abiding spiritual truth.

"Sure, the new hasn't worn off yet," Eric said. "And I love to talk about all the ways God keeps surprising me and challenging my comfort zone. But," and he paused for a second to get the words right, "I'd give anything to have the long-term knowledge, the deep familiarity, and the historic experience of God that you guys know and that you can draw on all the time."

"What do you mean?" Gary asked.

"Well, we've been studying the Gospel of John in here for the past few months," Eric explained. "So now I know John's story fairly well. But at the moment it's the only book in the Bible I'm anywhere near familiar with at all.

"You guys talk casually about people like Peter, Philip, and Nicodemus, or those Old Testament guys who lived in the desert. It's as if they're old friends and you know them or something. But I don't have all those hundreds of Sunday school stories to draw on, the kind of knowledge that takes years and years to sink in. I never sat around the Sunday dinner table with my family talking about church or picking at the preacher. This is my first real Bible study. I want to know more, I really do, but I feel like I'm so far behind that it's going to take years to catch up."

I understand exactly what Eric was talking about. But unfortunately—and certainly in respect to most of us around the table that day—he was talking about the culture of a religious upbringing rather than the ongoing practice of a deliberate spiritual life.

He really wasn't that far behind. To be honest, the unbounded desire of people like Eric often makes me feel embarrassed about my lackluster laissez-faire attitude, especially when I consider how poor a disciple I have been over the years. I've lived right slap in the middle of church since before I can remember, and yet I still don't have enough raw material engrafted into my subconscious from which to improvise with the degree of confidence that will be required if I'm ever going to take my spiritual life to the next level.

Four out of five ministers surveyed

OK, the correct number is more like "110 of 110 spiritual leaders interviewed," but ever since the series of classic commercials aired featuring the ubiquitous "four out of five dentists," I've had the image stuck in my head. The phrase "four out of five surveyed" has assumed a cache of gravitas I simply can't pass up.

I may not know a lot of dentists, but over the past three years I have interviewed well over one hundred Christian ministers and published almost as many news stories about their work. Without exception these spiritual leaders have always defined the process of spiritual formation directly in terms of our relationship to Christ.

One United Methodist leader said it well: "My growth as a Christian happens in direct proportion to my willingness to place myself in proximity to Jesus."

Yet at the same time the clerics were unequivocal regarding our need to be saturated with the Word of God. "Actually, that's one of the primary ways I get to know God," one Lutheran pastor told me. "God reveals his character specifically through the inspired words of the Bible. Sometimes when I read the Gospels it's like having Jesus himself sitting in an easy chair and sharing his heart with me one-on-one."

Who's in charge of our priorities?

"Kevin" sat across the breakfast table from me, pushing a lump of butter around the top of his pancakes with a fork. In his midthirties, he was married and up to his eyeballs in a long list of distractions that relentlessly pushed their way between him and everything of lasting value in his life.

Just to be sure we were both reading from the same page, I asked him to name the things he values most. He thought for a moment, then specified the following:

- His relationship with God
- His marriage
- His children
- His ability to truly enjoy the liberties we in the United States have taken so much for granted
- His home

There may be more, he said, but these were pretty much the top five. "So what's the problem?" I asked.

"It's like every time I turn on my brain, the only stuff that comes to the front is this pile of waste that's completely at odds with what I know I should have as my main concern," he said, obviously frustrated. "I'm a Christian; I've turned my life over to Christ. Why don't I wake up every morning with God's agenda stamped on my mind, front and center? If all I can think about is the other stuff, then maybe I'm not really that good a Christian. Sometimes I question if God even makes a difference."

So we talked about how much God values our individual freedom. This truth, I believe, is one of the coolest characteristics our Creator owns and a significant key to understanding how he shows his love and manages his intervention in our lives.

"God values our freedom so much that he chooses not to force himself into places and situations where he's not invited," I said. "If our idea of exactly where God belongs is limited to Sunday mornings—exclusively—then he is gracious enough to honor that restriction. Some of us have granted him Wednesday evening too. Fair enough."

God does not control Kevin's brain. Kevin controls his brain.

So I asked Kevin if he'd mind naming some things that distract him from following God. What elements and priorities constantly stymie his desire to pursue those things he knows would give him more genuine joy? I was referring to the stuff that stands in opposition to Paul's advice to his friends in Philippi:

> Whatever is true, whatever is honorable, whatever is just, whatever is pure, whatever is pleasing, whatever is commendable, if there is any excellence and if there is anything worthy of praise, think about these things. Keep on doing the things that you have learned and received and heard and seen in me, and the God of peace will be with you. (Phil. 4:8-9)

"Money," he said right off. "It's like I'm obsessed with it. I feel driven to make more money so that we can spend it on stuff I know in my heart will never make us happy. I end up working too much overtime, plus any number of Saturdays, and I even miss church sometimes. To be honest, I'm not really sure why I do it."

Kevin filled out the rest of his list for me. It wasn't pretty.

"How pathetic," he said when he was finished.

I've had similar conversations with other friends and even casual acquaintances, so I've consolidated a "Top Eight" list of false priorities that tend to get between Christian men and the things that really matter if we want to live authentic Christian lives in the twenty-first century.

1. *Money:* Or, as Jesus put it, "This is how it will be with anyone who stores up things for himself but is not rich toward God." (Luke 12:21, NIV)
2. *Stuff:* That would be large houses, cars, plasma televisions, and other toys.
3. *Prestige:* The desire to be recognized as a big shot by other people.
4. *Control:* Wanting to impose our will on those around us—including God.
5. *Sex:* That's everything from the Hooters billboard on the side of the road to Web sites we visit and what we think when the beautiful woman in the elevator says, "Good morning."
6. *Alcohol:* So how much of a priority is it, anyway?
7. *Television:* Sometimes it demands more of us than we are prepared to give to our relationships, including family.
8. *More:* More of anything—"I'll be satisfied when I have one more"; "This next promotion is it"; "If I could just upgrade the car one more time." Well, how is it going? Are we satisfied yet?

There's a question I always ask people like Kevin. And I ask it of myself too, pretty much every day: So who's in control here? Who calls the shots? Are we making our own decisions? Or have we handed that responsibility and opportunity over to someone else or some other entity?

Driving down the road the other day, I couldn't get this one song out of my head. I know you've had the experience. Usually it's a catchy little jingle that gets stuck in some kind of processing loop. I remember it happened with the song "It's a Small World" the last time Rebekah and I took our children to Disney World. Seemed like every other hour or so for two months the tune would run another irritating loop or two. After a few days I wanted to go back to the ride with a baseball bat and smack each of those little animated songsters in the head so I could put a permanent end to the relentless cycle!

It's amazing how readily we can retrieve so much detailed information from our subconscious minds. I can still narrate the entire Guinness beer commercial from around 1964 when it ran on our little black-and-white television set that overheated if it stayed plugged in much longer than an hour.

Why do certain ugly words and expressions come to our minds so easily in stressful situations? Most likely because we loaded the hopper with so many of them that some kind of automatic response is inevitable.

That's what was going on with my friend Kevin. He had been receiving such an overwhelming avalanche of messages that told him again and again where his priorities should reside. Commercials, movies, TV shows, conversations at work about sex, magazine articles, all manner of advertisements. . . . The list goes on, and the messages read like this:

"Buy, buy, buy! He who dies with the most toys wins."

"Casual sex is more fun and rewarding than committed love with your wife."

"Drinking large quantities of alcohol makes you confident, funny, and attractive—really it does. . . ."

"New and more powerful automobiles change your life."

"People with large plasma TVs are cooler and way more successful."

There's a lot more, but I think we all get the picture. It's kind of like the "It's a small world after all" song. The messages that we memorize through repetition and overexposure come back again and again.

OK, here's the heart of the question. He who controls the messages controls the person. So it's not a question of "Are we really influenced?" so much as a question of "Well then, who's going to be in charge of what influences me?"

An ongoing battle

The apostle Paul realized the importance of taking on the struggle with purpose and intention every day. Paul certainly was well aware of the tremendous resources the Christian man has at his disposal, but he was also savvy enough to name his enemy and to recognize the imperative of constant vigilance.

The structure and the value system of our world have evolved outside of God's promise for so long that it seems we are compelled to struggle against our very nature in order to follow Jesus. Like the highboard diver who must determine to overcome his reflexes each time he launches himself into the abyss, we must renew our decision for discipleship every single day. Then, also like the diver, we discover the cool, refreshing, life-giving waters and celebrate that what we have left behind is dryness and dust.

The skewed priorities of the culture we inhabit run deep. They are etched into the fabric of our decision-making processes and reinforced through a thousand messages and object lessons every day.

The morality of faithlessness and instant gratification pushes on our decision-making processes every time we engage the world on its terms. From pop-up ads to song lyrics to posters on the subway walls; from selfish drivers to a boss who lacks integrity and expects compromise; from the allure of another drink to the indecent propositions of a coworker. The world is broken and we live in it: end of story.

And so we dare not leave our faith at home or bottled up at church when we venture out. We dare not pretend that we can live the Christian life on our own. If Jesus had to say, "Not what I want but what you want" (Matt. 26:39), then how much more do we need the power of God's transforming presence in our day-to-day lives?

Paul writes the following in Romans 7:18-25:

> I know that nothing good dwells within me, that is, in my flesh. I can will what is right, but I cannot do it. For I do not do the good I want, but the evil I do not want is what I do. Now if I do what I do not want, it is no longer I that do it, but sin that dwells within me.
>
> So I find it to be a law that when I want to do what is good, evil lies close at hand. For I delight in the law of God in my inmost self, but I see in my members another law at war with the law of my mind, making me captive to the law of sin that dwells in my members. Wretched man that I am! Who will rescue me from this body of death? Thanks be to God through Jesus Christ our Lord!
>
> So then, with my mind I am a slave to the law of God, but with my flesh I am a slave to the law of sin.

Paul's dilemma should be familiar to each of us. Things can be pretty tough out there, and on the surface even this great man appears to be lamenting the inevitability of defeat. How can we possibly fight the overwhelming momentum of the way things are?

Good news and even better news for Christians

This is why any reading of the passage from Romans 7 should always be completed by taking a careful look at the opening verses found in the next chapter. The following declaration by Paul is an overwhelming testimony to victory in Christ:

> There is therefore now no condemnation for those who are in Christ Jesus. For the law of the Spirit of life in Christ Jesus has set you free from the law of sin and of death. For God has done what the law, weakened by the flesh, could not do. (Rom. 8:1-3)

OK, Paul seems to be saying, I certainly painted a fairly bleak picture when I talked about my ongoing battles with "the flesh." But that was my point. Through our own individual strength we can't win these kinds of battles. But that's all right, because we were not designed to live in that kind of isolation. We were specifically designed—from the ground up, if we read Genesis—to live in ongoing fellowship with God. If we want to talk about what is authentically "natural," then we simply have to get back to a fundamental dependence on God.

Put the law of the Spirit of life to work, providentially

This is what Paul is talking about when he writes about the opportunity we have to be transformed by the renewing of our minds. We already spent a little time discussing the concept of providence in a previous chapter. Providence, I suggested, is a crossroads—that compelling place where God's will and our choosing him work together.

Putting the law of the Spirit of life to work is all about providence. It means to deliberately and prayerfully choose to leverage the powerful principles of spiritual life to overcome the weakness of our natural flesh.

Consider, for example, the following challenge. What if you pledged to choose and memorize a fresh verse of scripture every morning while, say, brushing your teeth? Let's pretend. You're brushing your teeth now and going over John 15:15 from the New International Version. Jesus says: "I no longer call you servants, because a servant does not know his master's business. Instead, I have called you friends, for everything that I learned from my Father I have made known to you."

That's pretty wonderful stuff, right? So try repeating it, say, ten times while brushing your teeth and another ten times while getting dressed. Wait a minute or two, then quickly try to remember the words and say the verse out loud. Now it's stuck fairly well in your thoughts. Say it again as you open the car; then repeat the scripture a bunch more times instead of turning on the radio.

So what happens? For starters, you've got to be feeling pretty great. I mean, Jesus—the Savior of the world—wants to think of you and me as his friends. That's amazingly powerful stuff. What you have achieved through this short exercise, in effect, is the seeding of a new and trans-formational thought into the first level of consciousness that you carry into the day.

Here's what can happen. Some bad, naughty—see, I didn't say "moronic"—driver cuts you off in traffic before launching a very rude gesture in your direction. Miracle of miracles, instead of a curse word leaping into your brain, you find yourself repeating the following: "I no longer call you servants, because a servant does not know his mas-ter's business. Instead, I have called you friends, for everything that I learned from my Father I have made known to you."

Before you know it, you're talking with God again, maybe praying for the other driver, maybe asking God to guide your thoughts, cer-tainly understanding the power of God's awesome Word to transform us by the renewing of our minds.

Here's how the apostle Paul worded the idea. This passage is revo-lutionary so far as psychology is concerned, especially considering that he wrote these words all the way back in the first century AD:

> Do not be conformed to this world, but be transformed by the
> renewing of your minds, so that you may discern what is the will of
> God—what is good and acceptable and perfect. (Rom. 12:2)

7   FiNDiNG A BAND OF BROTHERS

Let us consider how to provoke one another to love and good deeds, not neglecting to meet together, as is the habit of some, but encouraging one another.

—Hebrews 10:24-25

Pat Patterson is one of my spiritual mentors. He was less than enthusiastic, however, when I first suggested he get involved with small-group Bible study and spiritual growth experiences designed exclusively for men.

"It will never fly," he said. "You won't be able to get men to meet together to pray for each other and study the Bible. They'll be lost without at least a few women in the mix to keep things focused. The experience will be surface-level at best and quite likely a complete flop."

Pat's point of view fit in with the generally unchallenged notion that men as a gender are simply not capable of engaging other men in meaningful dialogue, that men are destined to be categorically uninterested in serious spiritual formation—especially if it involves talking about anything other than sports . . . or maybe cars . . . or possibly business, but otherwise the conversation is doomed to drag.

Getting men to participate, conventional wisdom declares, would be like pulling teeth and probably less rewarding than, say, a nice lengthy IRS audit.

But I didn't buy it. First, I like a challenge. Tell me something isn't possible, and right away I'll be interested. Second, I have formed a general thesis that Christianity at its best is necessarily countercultural, and that theory is especially true when it comes to the role of men. Maybe the best reason to go ahead with an idea is when the protocols of the-way-things-are say no. Besides, I felt an urgency inside me that was nudging me forward and not likely to give up. It simply had to be the Holy Spirit.

So I took a look around at the friends I hung out with at church and at work. They were all-American guys, baby boomers—fellow travelers on what felt like a new road. They were the kind of men Jesus would make a beeline for if he was looking for—and he is—a new group of faithful disciples today. I've listed some of their characteristics below:

1. To a man they all were motivated to do well in their careers.
2. Mostly they tended to let their wives carry the conversation when talk turned to spiritual matters or anything related to feelings.
3. Their worship attendance was spotty, and their participation in ministry teams was less than stellar. The church had learned not to expect much from my friends; consequently, they did their best to deliver.
4. They loved to talk about sports, cars, and business.
5. But they also loved to talk about their children; they were honest in their desire to know more about God; and they were not closed off to owning their emotions. They felt deeply about their families; they loved God sincerely; and they were willing to grow as people.
6. Additionally, they were not saddled with the same oppressive weight of cultural chauvinism that had so effectively strictured their parents' generation.
7. Finally, the majority of the men who occupied my circle already strongly suspected that the Jesus they were beginning to know— however superficially—was indeed much more of a bona fide man than the emotionally constipated image of a "real man" promoted via the doctrines of machismo, the prejudices of religion, and the lack of imagination demonstrated by the status quo.

At face value the first four points may well have confirmed Pat's conclusion, but the balance of the list effectively revealed the real potential for an entirely different story.

So I launched the first "Men's Room" and gently introduced my friends to the idea of spiritual formation and interpersonal accountability in the context of deliberate Christian community.

The time was right

The concept took off immediately. We had enough for two groups; we met every Wednesday; and the men's wives could not have been happier. (Some of the guys were suspicious about their wives being so happy, but once they realized the experience also enhanced their communication skills at home—across the board—then the men were very happy too!)

Before long my mentor Pat was completely won over. "I'm so glad you didn't listen to me when I said this wouldn't work," he said.

"It's absolutely wonderful to see the growth that happens to these men," Pat told me later. "It means so much to me. Right in front of my eyes I see something I'm not able to explain by the normal senses: God's Spirit working in our midst."

Twenty-first-century man is not an island

I hate to break it to those of us who like to exercise worn stereotypes, but women are not the only gender to have benefited from the social revolutions of the past thirty years. Like it or not, John Wayne is long gone; sometimes manly men really do just need to have a good cry; and the idea that strong silent men are supposed to "Bite the bullet and just get the job done, by golly, because we don't ask for help from anyone . . ." is not only pathetically inappropriate but fundamentally contrary to God's best intention for our lives.

Men who want to grow in Christlike grace need one another.

Men who intend to be the kind of followers Christ empowers through his strength and love more often than not discover their purpose and their power in community.

Besides, we were created specifically for relationship, relationship with God and with one another. We were created for communion with God and with other men. Being alone runs contrary to the most primary and basic intention of creation.

Jesus found himself a small group

Jesus may be God Incarnate, Lord of all creation, Emmanuel, Wonderful Counselor, Prince of Peace, Coming Messiah, Light of life, and so on, but the Master himself deliberately engaged his public ministry here on earth by surrounding himself with a small covenant group of other men who knew and loved God. How much more should we place ourselves in the company of fellow believers?

Jesus is our model and our guide. Understanding and committing to the same spiritual disciplines the Master found important in his ministry among us is no small potatoes. There's no way we can close our eyes to Christ's precedent: finding companions for the journey is huge.

PhD-level growth as disciples

My discipleship group is built on four essential elements: my prayerful preparation, participation in an accountability team (my church uses the ChristCare Series® developed by Stephen Ministries), reading God's Word, and the use of well-thought-out questions to drive heartfelt and beneficial discussion.

A sense of shared commitment and purpose in such a group can make all the difference. The discussion is great, our fellowship is excellent, and praying for one another can be life-changing. But something even more remarkable tends to happen when a dozen or so guys bring open spirits, humble hearts, and keen, incisive minds to the same table.

I call it "PhD-level Bible study." Let me explain.

Traditionally, in academia, the bachelor's degree is awarded to students based on their exposure to a broad curriculum of learning with particular emphasis in one discipline—a major field of study such as chemistry, foreign languages, math, or English. A master's degree is earned when postgraduate students demonstrate mastery in their chosen field of study. The doctorate (PhD) supposedly represents the next level, a step beyond mastery. Doctoral candidates must prove to a dissertation committee that they have actually created new knowledge, covering ground previously uncharted in their highly specialized field.

Here's why I say a small discipleship group can be called PhD-level Bible study. When a group of hungry hearts engages God's Word with deliberate humility, the author of the text always comes through. When men ask God to be present as an active participant in the discussion, consciously allowing the Holy Spirit to speak, the result of such conversation tends to be greater than the sum of each individual contribution.

This has been my experience, time after time. When the guys I gather with study scripture and proceed to share honestly how God is working in their lives, something profound and illuminating always emerges. Sometimes we find that Paul's admonition in Romans 12 bears out, and we truly are transformed through the renewing of our minds.

When that happens, new insight emerges. Stuff nobody knew before we sat down together that evening. Truth that God lays on our hearts through the ministry of the Holy Spirit and the revelation of God's Word.

That's what I call PhD-level Bible study. Something that's only possible when we sign on with others to grow together in our knowledge and our faith.

Changed into his likeness

A verse in 2 Corinthians 3 talks about how God works to help us to grow spiritually. "All of us, with unveiled faces, seeing the glory of the Lord as though reflected in a mirror, are being transformed into the same image from one degree of glory to another; for this comes from the Lord, the Spirit" (v. 18).

Commitment to Christian discipleship in the context of a small group is one way we can spend quality time with Jesus. When we do, we are changed.

These are some of the primary ways we can know God:

1. The revelation of his character through the Bible
2. The incarnation of his love in the person of Jesus Christ
3. The experience of his presence through prayer
4. The power of his presence in the Holy Spirit
5. The fellowship of his body—the church
6. The mystery and the joy experienced through worship
7. Natural revelation, the witness of the creation to the Creator

Meeting together with other Christian men for prayer and Bible study places us close to God. The passage in 2 Corinthians suggests that spending time in the presence of God is a key element to spiritual transformation. What is spiritual growth if it is not being transformed into the image of the Lord?

In 2 Corinthians 3 the apostle Paul recalls Moses's experience when he returned from meeting with God on the mountain. God's presence passed over Moses, and it was a dangerous situation. God had told Moses, "While my glory passes by I will put you in a cleft of the rock, and I will cover you with my hand until I have passed by; then I will take away my hand, and you shall see my back; but my face shall not be seen" (Exod. 33:22-23).

Consequently, when Moses returned to the children of Israel, his face shone so brightly that they couldn't stand the light. "The Israelites would see the face of Moses, that the skin of his face was shining; and Moses would put the veil on his face again, until he went in to speak with him" (Exod. 34:35). Moses had to wear a veil in order to protect the people from the tiny remnant of twice-removed glory he carried in his countenance.

Because of Jesus, Paul points out, we do not have to see God's glory through a veil. Indeed, we have direct access, and because of that we certainly will be changed.

The danger of transformation

What a lot of people miss is that engaging the presence of God has not become any less dangerous since the days of Moses.

The danger, of course, is that God will change us.

That's why some of us don't pray so much. There's a great story from The Men's Room that illustrates this point. I'll refer to it again in chapter 12 when we talk about daring to follow Jesus.

My men's group is characteristically extremely honest when we share around the table. Honesty is a necessary prelude to transformation. The guys just lay their thoughts and feelings in the open. Nothing facilitates spiritual growth much more effectively than the habit of telling the truth.

A prime example is the day we were batting around a challenge in regard to our personal prayer life.

"I'm suggesting that we all select a clearly defined topic for prayer," I said. "It could be your relationship with your wife, a temptation you need to deal with, the direction of your career—anything God places on your mind. We won't ask for anything specific, not a request per se, but instead we will simply lay ourselves open to God. Then we can plan to report in every week and share with the group exactly how God is challenging us and what we are doing—or not doing—in response."

Darrell is fairly new to taking God that seriously, so he felt the need to share some of his caution and air his questions with the group.

"Let me get this straight," he said. "What we're talking about here is asking God for direction in our lives, right? Kind of letting God take more active control?"

"That's right," someone said. "We have to be open to God's leading and see where it takes us. Sounds like a good exercise."

"Exercise, nothing! What it sounds like to me is dangerous!" Darrell said. "Listen. The way I'm used to praying is like this: I tell God what I want him to do, then God either gets on board with my agenda, or he doesn't. Simple enough."

He looked around the room. "We're talking about letting God lead us. We're talking about God calling the shots. You know, I'm sorry, guys, but I'm not so sure that I'm ready to give God that kind of latitude in my life."

I love Darrell.

What can you do in the presence of honesty like that but grow spiritually? Darrell knew what was at stake, probably more clearly than those of us who tend to make such prayers too routine or perfunctory. So he didn't let the rest of us soft-shoe around the obvious with holy language and halfhearted commitments.

If we say it, my friend reasoned, then we should mean it. Otherwise why bother saying it at all?

Later, once Darrell was ready to give God the kind of latitude that such a commitment to change requires, well, let me tell you . . .

Covenant and accountability

Men who want to grow and to move forward do best when they can drum up a little accountability. Or, if the word *accountability* sounds too invasive or potentially harsh, we can talk about company, fellow travelers, companions on the journey.

Once our "Men's Room prayer challenge" was on the table, so was our accountability to one another. Our group, you see, is a covenant group. That means we have agreed to keep certain promises, and we hold one another accountable to the covenant.

Here are some of the items our covenant usually covers:

1. We respect confidentiality.
2. We are honest and straightforward.
3. We promise to attend faithfully and to let someone know if we can't make it to a meeting.
4. We agree to keep up with the assigned reading each week.

5. We promise to pray for one another daily and encourage one
   another during the week.
6. We respect one another's points of view.
7. We may have a wide range of political opinions—indeed, we run
   the gamut—but our emphasis together is Jesus and how being a
   Christian disciple can transform our day-to-day lives.
8. We agree to work on ongoing mission projects on behalf of our
   church.
9. We listen actively.
10. We love unconditionally.

Love one another as I have loved you

Love is incredibly liberating for men who are learning to be countercultural about the impact of personal faith on the world and their community. What we have found—and this discovery has taken us a little
by surprise—is that it's impossible *not* to love the people you pray and
share burdens with on a regular basis.

"But wait," you say. "This is a men's group we're talking about here;
don't start to get all lovey-dovey on me now."

Remember, we have been talking about the fact that Jesus calls us
to be different than the norm, especially in terms of the world we live
in. If we want to follow Jesus, we will have to seriously consider being
somewhat revolutionary when it comes to a lot of standard church culture as well.

Jesus was clear and direct about love and its expression among
those he called friends: "I give you a new commandment, that you love
one another. Just as I have loved you, you also should love one another.
By this everyone will know that you are my disciples, if you have love
for one another" (John 13:34-35).

Paul picked up Christ's theme in his letter to the Romans: "Love
one another with mutual affection; outdo one another in showing
honor" (12:10). The honor is for others—because of love—and honor
is not something Jesus wants us to grasp for ourselves.

That's not exactly the way our culture tends to operate, is it? But then
this particular band of brothers has committed to follow Jesus instead.

DEVOTION

8   THE LONG, DEEP BREATH

> The Advocate, the Holy Spirit, whom the Father will send in my
> name, will teach you everything, and remind you of all that I
> have said to you. Peace I leave with you; my peace I give to you.
> I do not give to you as the world gives. Do not let your hearts be
> troubled, and do not let them be afraid.
>
> —*John 14:26-27*

I talk with a lot of people. It's what I do. I interview them for newspaper articles, pick their brains over breakfast or lunch, and work the crowd after church. I sift for ideas, ask hard questions, and follow up fortuitous openings. Conversations tend to go much deeper than people anticipate, but almost always they are glad that they did.

The collective wisdom that emerges from the ongoing conversation I enjoy with members of my adult Sunday school class inspires me; the dialogue that emerges in response to my op-ed column can get interesting in a hurry; the insight small-group leaders demonstrate in supervision sometimes knocks my socks off. I ask people what they think about matters of faith; I ask them about their personal relationship with God. I listen, nod a lot, think about what they share, and—always—I learn.

My research methodology may be unscientific, but the anecdotal evidence I have collected tells me that fewer than ten of every one hundred Christian men I talk with have an active, well-considered daily devotional life. That's a really low number.

But here's a piece of completely reliable corollary data that turns out to be remarkably interesting: 100 percent of those who do maintain a regular devotional discipline report that the daily routine pays off in ways that are nothing short of miraculous.

By miraculous I mean eternal, unremitting, awesome, satisfying, and unarguably life-changing. By miraculous I also mean a discernible improvement in their daily lives across the board. Relationships, parenting, work attitude, productivity, work satisfaction, effective Christian witness, love life—need I go on? This is true even when the men I talk with believe they are just beginning to scratch the surface regarding their daily walk with God. The investment of just a few short but deliberate minutes, every day, makes a difference in the lives of Christian men that cannot be accounted for by any other variable.

If any advertised manufactured product could claim anywhere near the level and consistency of the verifiable results found in consequence of a daily devotional life, that product would sell off the shelves. We're aware of the benefits. So what holds us back?

How to fall in love with God

Our personal day-by-day experience of worship and prayer marks a distinct element of spiritual formation where both discipleship and devotion are spoken in the same breath.

Our commitment to daily prayer, worship, and study is a key element in the ongoing decision to be a disciple of Jesus.

The same activity is also one of the most reliable ways to fall in love with God.

The long, deep breath

During my other life, back when I was a schoolteacher, I used to refer to dedicated, deliberate moments with God as "my long, deep breath."

Starting the morning by taking a quiet time with God was certainly a good beginning to my day. However, as each day progressed, I realized that the more often I scheduled interludes of thoughtful fellowship with Jesus, the more effective I was in the classroom.

In other words, if I wanted to transform lives, then I had to start—and then continue—with my own.

My particular specialty was in working with children diagnosed with extreme behavior disorders and with students who were emotionally disturbed on a variety of levels. I also spent several years teaching autistic students.

Depending on the school district, my kids wore labels such as EH (emotionally handicapped), BD (behavior disordered), and SED (severely emotionally disturbed). In laymen's terms, these were the kids who threw other children through classroom windows, cursed more eloquently than gangsters, attacked teachers with desks and baseball bats, fought at the drop of a hat, lost contact with reality, tore books and papers into small shreds, and spit in principals' faces. At least that's the shorter, more technical description.

I remember doing my best to drive to work in calmness and serenity, enjoying the ride in with my windows down and roof open. I'd listen to some classic Eagles, maybe James Taylor, mellow and in the groove, then roll into the parking lot relaxed and happy, with my guard completely down. I'd walk nonchalantly across the grassy playing fields, say hi to some of my colleagues, and pour a satisfying cup of coffee.

Then, suddenly, without warning, a deep black hole would open up and suck me into its dark vortex. Remember Dorothy, Toto, and the farmhouse spinning uncontrollably toward Oz? Or maybe the destruction of the Death Star at the end of *Return of the Jedi*? Yes, often it was just like that. Another scene that comes to mind is the kidnapping episode in *Sleeping Beauty*. The hero, Prince Phillip, opens the door to the old cottage in the woods only to be ambushed by the evil Maleficent and her hoards of ghouls, trolls, and goblins. Arriving at work was sometimes a lot like that, only more so.

I remember one particular day when I was working as the crisis teacher and reading specialist in day treatment at the community mental health center. I hadn't taken more than a couple of small sips of that delightfully aromatic coffee before I ran into my boss.

"Morning, Derek," he began. "We have three teachers attending a workshop on the other side of town, and the substitutes are all new, so please make sure to keep an eye on their rooms—especially since two of these classrooms won't have their teacher's aides today. You might want to go directly to Mrs. Lentil's room, because Kevin and Walter have already started to go off the deep end, and she's not even there yet— something about a fender bender on the way in, I think. . . ."

He inhaled quickly and launched into his second gasp before I could think of a creative response. "Anyway, you'll have to cover for me during the two emergency staffing conferences because I have that thing after lunch, and I've already told the other teachers to talk to you if anything difficult comes up after 8:00 this morning because I have a meeting . . ."

He was putting on his coat, dialing his phone, and slipping out the door before I could muster anything even vaguely helpful to fend off the inevitable onslaught of chaos.

"Oh," he called over his shoulder, "Sammy's mother is really upset about something—I'm sure you remember her because you helped fill out the police report last time. I thought I should let you know she's waiting in your room, and she has some guy with her who says he's the boy's uncle."

Dazed, I stepped into the hallway only to have my coffee knocked out of my hand by Johnny, who was literally bouncing off the walls. Mr. Green, the eighth-grade teacher, poked his head around the corner. "Hey, Derek," he said, "I'm glad you've got Johnny in hand there. He's been wrecking my classroom, and he can't come back until he's calmed down enough and cleaned up the mess he made in the boys' bathroom. Thanks."

"No," I replied, "thank *you*."

And off he went. And off I went. I took care of Johnny's little attitude problem with maybe a tad more directive encouragement than he would normally have received from a calm guy like me. Then I plunged headlong into my day, thankful that I had no immediate crisis of my own to worry about and grateful for the coffee that had remained in my mug. I performed mental gymnastics to schedule my morning, ready for anything. It turns out that it's just as well that I was.

I could describe the way Joseph took a baseball bat and relocated a number of potted plants, or the way Porter talked about my grandmother—and he doesn't even know her. Or maybe I could describe what Danny and Ryan did to their classroom and that poor, defenseless substitute teacher whom I imagined we would never see again. But I think I've painted a fairly clear picture.

Anyway, by around 9:30 things began to settle down somewhat, and I managed to get a few things accomplished, another cup of coffee poured, and at least a handle on what was happening—a chance at last to catch my breath.

It was certainly a good thing that I had started out my day with a short devotional moment. I had spent fifteen minutes humming my favorite hymn while walking a mile and then praying about the coming day on my way home. But I needed the considered and practiced presence of Christ there in the musty hallway outside the school office where I was dealing with one more in a series of difficult and potentially dangerous teenagers.

It was only a long, deep breath, but I took it in gradually, breathing the name of Jesus. I held that good Christ-laden air in for a slow count of at least five seconds before releasing it, measured and deliberate—and in doing so I breathed the beginnings of a prayer. "Give me strength for this moment, Lord; please help me to represent the presence of Christ in the lives of those around me."

Sometimes it's easy to become concerned and overwhelmed when considering the locus of control in our lives, especially when faced day in, day out with the kind of situations I have described. It's easy to feel that everything is cool and mellow and balanced when it is just me, flying solo, quietly in control of my destiny. But then everything else hits the fan and—bingo!—I've lost my cool, my mellowness, my balance, and I may even forget that I'm a Christian.

Sometimes it's our own children.
Sometimes it's the boss.
Sometimes it's our spouse.
Sometimes it's the customers.
Sometimes it's the traffic.
Always it's ourselves.

Often it's a cumulative effect, and we suddenly realize that we are crowded in, pushed around, unable to feel personally in control of who we are and what we are feeling. Whatever is going on, it is very unsettling and not at all conducive, we feel, either to spiritual growth or our desire to share our faith with the world around us through living victorious lives.

But then maybe what is going on turns out to be exactly conducive, because all of the craziness and the difficulties that define reality point to the need for something that will overcome defeat. Because that is exactly the place where victory comes into play—if our faith is to have any credibility at all—and when most of the curious and the doubtful just happen to be looking in.

The answer is to stop.

Stop, even if only for thirty seconds. And while we are taking those several long, deep, cleansing breaths that science already tells us will reduce stress physically, we can think about whose children we are—God's. We can think about what mission we are on—to add light and peace to a hurting world. And we can pray for God's serenity to flow in, and through, and because of, our lives of discipleship and deliberate devotion.

Now, this won't change the fact of the particular situation we are engaging at the time. But the long, deep breath most certainly changes our relationship to such events; it absolutely will change us; and it may well affect the final outcome.

We confirm our identity as Christian men who desire to follow Jesus in every decision we make. We strengthen it through our attention to the details of becoming Jesus' disciples. And that identity becomes increasingly and powerfully transformational as we incorporate devotion into the fabric of our day-to-day lives.

Victory and more

We are children of the living God. If we can keep that simple truth central in our hearts and minds, we will live victorious lives.

I'm talking about incorporating our devotion into the routine of conscious thought. Not only will we know victory, but also we will experience the joy of becoming ambassadors of grace.

Not only ambassadors of grace, but people who will never need to be afraid. We will panic less often; we will waste less time and money; and we will become whole people. We will know more of God's peace; we will change the world.

I speak the truth

As I said, I talk with a lot of people. But don't just take my word for it. Have a little chat about your devotional life with God himself. After that, be deliberate. Set an hourly alarm if you have to, and then spend a minute or two practicing the long, deep breath of devotion, no matter what you're doing at the time.

You've seen the disclaimers they slap on those television advertisements? "Results may vary." "Results not typical." "Do not attempt unless under a doctor's supervision." Well, the commitment to a deliberate life of devotion should come with a different set of addendums:

"Warning: this practice is guaranteed to change your life." "God is faithful and true." "Don't pray if you don't want to grow."

Also, we should certainly take care not to spend such deliberate and thoughtful time with God unless we are mindful of what might happen if we begin to love him. Love is a powerful witness. Men who love God are a force to be reckoned with.

TO KNOW JESUS IS TO LOVE HIM

[Jesus] said to him, "'You shall love the Lord your God with all your heart, and with all your soul, and with all your mind.'"

—*Matthew 22:37*

When they had finished breakfast, Jesus said to Simon Peter, "Simon son of John, do you love me more than these?" He said to him, "Yes, Lord; you know that I love you." Jesus said to him, "Feed my lambs."

—*John 21:15*

Her name was Mrs. White, and she spoke passionately about her work among the desperate and the poor in India. Retiring after a lifetime of service, she had a million stories to share. She showed some slides, read from the scriptures, told some stories, and touched a lot of hearts. The speaking tour was a kind of valedictory, one last opportunity to spread the news and to raise consciousness about the amazing work of the church going on halfway around the world.

Many in the congregation that evening were inspired. They wrote checks, gathered information, renewed their personal enthusiasm for missions, and added the important legacy of the retired missionary to their ongoing commitment in prayer. Some even felt led by the Holy Spirit to consider a calling to work overseas.

"Mrs. White," one man said as he stood up during question time, "you must love India very deeply. I'm sure you're going to miss that part of the world now that you have returned to the United States. I know it's going to be very hard for you."

"Not at all," she smiled ruefully. "I hated every minute of it. India is the filthiest, most corrupt place I have ever seen. The people I worked with were disease-ridden and desperate. The conditions were deplorable.

I lost my husband and one child to that terrible place. If I never go back to India this side of eternity, it will be one day too soon."

The silence in the church was deafening. The congregation was stunned, and the man who asked the question just stood there with his mouth hanging open. Everyone wondered if the wiry old lady with a kick in her attitude had maybe lost her mind.

"But," she continued, after a theatrical pause, "for the sake of the love of Jesus I would go back there tomorrow."

Tears rolled down the elderly missionary's sun-wrinkled cheeks, and she gripped the sides of the podium tightly. Mrs. White fairly glowed with the radiance of devotion.

It wasn't humanitarianism that drove her life's work; it wasn't the lure or romanticism of overseas service; and it wasn't even a deep, abiding affection for the people she served that had ripened and matured over time. It was Jesus whom she loved and served. A deep, authentic love for God gave real teeth to Mrs. White's commitment to be a disciple, and this love moved her from contemplation out into the world.

Love trumps law

Over the past few chapters we have looked at the decisions we are making to become active disciples of Jesus Christ. What can we learn? How can we learn? Who can we learn with? How does the decision for discipleship advance our spiritual lives?

When the Pharisees cornered Jesus and asked him a question about the law—the old covenant (Matt. 22:34-40), he eloquently pointed out the next and most profound truth we need to understand if we are going to grow at all spiritually.

Our discipline and learning may be important elements in becoming mature spiritual beings, but no ingredient of the law, not even a small particle, does us much good at all outside the context of love. Christ's elegant summation in Matthew 22 serves to transition our discussion from discipleship into devotion: "Love the Lord your God completely; love God with all your heart; love God with all your soul; and love God with your entire mind," Jesus instructed. "Then, if you extend that love to the world around you and especially to your neighbors, you effectively address everything covered in the law and the prophets" (vv. 36-40, author's paraphrase).

Love trumps law, Jesus said. Love completes law. Love fulfills law. What we are finding out, through the grace of God and via our fellowship with other believers, is the fact that purposeful discipleship can lead us into devotion. Law and grace are indeed closely related, but not in the way the legalists would have us think.

Enlist heart, soul, and mind if we want to grow

When Jesus was asked to make a judgment regarding the most important aspect of a life of faith, he was characteristically unequivocal.

It's all quite straightforward, Jesus told the Pharisees (as if they really wanted to know). All you have to remember is the law of love. "Love the Lord your God with all your heart, and with all your soul, and with all your mind."

Love for God—in Jesus' assessment, all-encompassing love that extends all the way to the core of who we are—is critical if we want a spiritual life that will mean anything or progress anywhere at all.

But men don't get all emotional!

But we aren't simply Christians; we're Christian men. Love at that level is a little harder for us to embrace.

We all know how men are. Men don't go for all that namby-pamby love stuff. We like to punch one another in the arm, make disparaging remarks about each other, barbeque together, insult one another's golf game, maybe exchange a few slaps on the back. We're all about high fives and handshakes. And while we're on the subject of handshakes, of course I mean good, firm, manly ones. None of this fish-hand nonsense, two hands cupped over another man's hand, or a handshake that lingers too long and makes both of us feel uncomfortable.

So I know where a lot of us are coming from. There comes a point, however, where our spiritual life will come to a standstill unless we manage, quite literally, to fall in love with Jesus.

It's time to step up

In the final analysis, gender stereotypes (no matter how tempting they are for those of us who try to measure up to our culture's value system) serve to isolate both men and women from real spiritual growth. But men especially, because so many of us have been hoodwinked into believing that emotion somehow threatens our core identity. That's because an enormous amount of our cultural perspective equates strength with control, and if our sense of self-worth is vested in the cultural model, then we dare not fall in love with God.

This is what is known in theological circles as "hooey!" We were created in God's image, and our emotions are a part of the package. We really can't deny them without—in effect—rejecting the image of God.

Last week I cried in church

> While they were eating, [Jesus] took a loaf of bread, and after blessing it he broke it, gave it to them, and said, "Take; this is my body." Then he took a cup, and after giving thanks he gave it to them, and all of them drank from it. He said to them, "This is my blood of the covenant, which is poured out for many. Truly I tell you, I will never again drink of the fruit of the vine until that day when I drink it new in the kingdom of God." (Mark 14:22-25)

Sometimes while the bread and the wine are being served during Communion, I play background music along with my friends Mark and Nathan. One Sunday earlier this year we simply played a series of arrangements around the central theme of "Amazing Grace." Then God's spirit took me completely by surprise: I was completely overwhelmed with love. You have to understand that Mark's piano playing is sensitive and worshipful—he tickles the ivories as if they were an extension of his soul, and Nathan can lay out a bluesy line on his acoustic guitar reminiscent of Chet Atkins. As for me, I'm just along for the ride, but what a privilege and a joy to be able to play along.

Apart from the beauty of the music, however, I found myself lost in the words and in the deep meaning bound up in "Amazing Grace." I watched the people I love taking the bread that represents Christ's broken body and drinking the grape juice that signifies the blood of Jesus spilled willingly for us in such agony and in the face of such complete rejection.

Christ not only offers us the cup, but he drinks from it too. Back when Jesus lived in Palestine, Hebrew families often participated in a moving ceremony designed to confirm the decision of a man and a woman to marry. The man and his father would come to the home of the woman's family to talk about the proposed betrothal. Once terms were agreed upon, wine would be prepared, and the potential groom would pour a glass of wine before offering the cup to the young woman in question. Once she accepted the cup and took a drink of the wine, the purposeful gesture meant that she accepted the full commitment of marriage and all that such a far-reaching decision might entail. Or, as was her right, the woman could decline; she could let the cup pass. In that case, the contract would not, could not, be activated.

Here is the imagery that somehow presented itself in my mind that Sunday morning while I was playing "Amazing Grace" on the guitar and watching the people I love take Communion. Jesus, in the garden of Gethsemane, after leaving the communion of the Last Supper and praying fervently for his followers, voiced the following prayer: "Abba, Father, for you all things are possible; remove this cup from me; yet, not what I want, but what you want" (Mark 14:36).

Jesus took the cup and drank from it, even though he knew exactly what would happen next. His commitment to me resembles the promise of marriage. "I'm in," Jesus was saying. "I'm in because I love you enough not only to spill my own blood for you but enough to remain committed to you for all eternity. Nothing left behind, no holdout; you have all there is of me. I'm drinking from this cup."

There in church, playing the guitar in front of three hundred people, I found myself crying. Tears streamed down my face, and I couldn't even wipe my sleeve across my eyes. It was love, love for Jesus and a realization of what exactly he has done for me. I'll admit that I was embarrassed, and I wanted so badly to pretend I was coughing so I could reach for my handkerchief. But I believe God knew that I needed the opportunity to show my love without holding back. To be honest, I'm glad it happened. It's one of those hurdles I've managed to get beyond. I pray that I will never again be ashamed of my love.

As men we simply must catch this spirit

I am privileged to belong to an exhilarating congregation defined by vitality, renewal, laughter, prayer, growth, deep joy, and—not coincidentally—more young families and children than we know what to do with.

A key demographic, I believe, and one that statistical analysis rarely cites, is that of active male participation. The commitment level of men amounts to a key measurement that can effectively predict the spiritual health of the whole congregation. Simply put, a community of faith with active men is a church experiencing reengagement of spiritual life across the board.

Yes, I'm talking about men actually excited about church. I'm talking about men who are willing to move their discipleship into the realm of devotion. I'm talking about men who love Jesus and are not afraid to say so.

I honestly believe that the amazing health and vibrancy I witness week by week at my home church directly relates to the balance of enthusiasm and commitment both women and men bring to the faith community. Men and women working together to advance God's kingdom—that is what God intends. If the women—by and large—are already on board, then I guess it's time for us men to step up.

That means it's time to let go of our pride and to love Jesus. Once we let down that barrier, the rest, as they say, will be history.

Jesus redefines "man's man"

The call to discipleship for men is simply a call to follow Jesus. It is a call to love Christ and to honestly engage our emotions. It is a call to fall in love with God without trying to disguise our feelings because we are embarrassed by "weakness" or tears.

I happen to be a good athlete, but sometimes the rampant use of "manly" sports metaphors for men's spirituality disturbs me. Yes, we're men, but I really don't believe it does our witness much good to adopt language and practices that pay more homage to the testosterone-saturated culture of machismo than our fundamental need to know Jesus and to grow spiritually.

Christ's message is revolutionary, and it does not necessarily have to speak the exact language of our culture. Instead, we should learn the language of Jesus, the language of love. The thrust of the New Testament witness cannot—indeed should not—be neatly repackaged in clichéd "man-friendly" terms. In the same vein, Christ's message is most definitely not a subset of any political ideology. That includes Democrats, Republicans, and any other party we can imagine.

Jesus is looking for men who are willing to follow him. But I am concerned that too many of us—both Christians and those who are seeking—have been given the impression that we should either go along with the locker room huddle for Jesus, or we have no other alternative.

I'm here to say that Jesus is highly motivated and anxious to get back into the hearts and lives of moderate American men who want to serve him at church, at home, at work, and in the balance of everything they do.

Christ is saying—loud and clear, I believe—that he loves us and wants us to love him enough to move forward in a spiritual walk that will change this nation through the day-to-day lives of ordinary men called to follow in his way. Ordinary men, of course, become extraordinary men when they follow Jesus and respond to the imperative of his truth.

Jesus will empower and use us to further his kingdom whatever our political persuasion, denominational affiliation, or status in life. Whether our proclivity is to love the outdoors, to eat and drink professional sports, to read romantic poetry, or to simply play all weekend with our children.

It doesn't matter. What matters is that we need to fall in love with Jesus.

A man who loves Jesus

I recently interviewed a pastor while preparing a story for the local newspaper. As always, the visit was positive, and I enjoyed the meeting on many levels. We talked about his family, his career, his relationship to the community, the old Florida he grew up in as a child, and the church he had built and loved so deeply.

Then I asked the pastor about Jesus. I asked him about what still motivates him to keep on preaching after all this time, and I asked him why the message he delivers on Sunday should have anything at all to do with the day-to-day balance of our lives.

"Let me tell you about Jesus," he said. And immediately his eyes filled with tears. He shared the simple testimony of how Jesus connected with his humble life and called him into service, and how his Savior remains so profoundly linked to every moment of his every day, and he couldn't help but let the tears flow.

"I'm sorry about the tears," he said. "But I can't talk about Jesus without being affected this way. I just love him so much."

He was an old "Florida cracker" who used to work as a superintendent for an oil company. He knew how to handle himself. He was all man all the way through. Yet the love of Jesus touched his heart and his soul so deeply that it still brought tears to his eyes.

Such deep love for Jesus is the key to spiritual growth and the way we move ever closer to God.

So do we love Jesus?

One reason spiritual life is so vibrant at my church is because we have so many men who aren't afraid to show their deep love for Jesus. "The Holy Spirit is loose in this church," my good friend Jerry said one Sunday. That's what happens when both women and men have the courage to let go of their cultural inhibitions and allow themselves to be touched personally by a living Savior.

Things haven't always been that way. Indeed, a decade ago the number of faithful and active men involved was disappointingly low and mostly limited to those over fifty. As a community of faith our corporate spiritual growth was significantly stunted. You could walk into the sanctuary on Sunday morning, and all you could feel was the presence of hungry people waiting for something that wasn't happening. Good people, yes, but there was little sense of vitality, no powerful rush of spiritual energy, and scant evidence of the abundant joy to be found when we claim and embrace our love for Jesus.

So one day, as part of a series of messages designed to set a new direction and to connect with the heart of what is basic and essential about our lives as spiritual beings, my wife, Rebekah, preached a sermon titled "Do You Love Jesus?"

Evidently she caused quite a stir. Early the next day a gentleman wielding a lot of political clout strode into her office and demanded, "What do you mean by asking us if we love Jesus?"

"It's a good question," she responded. "So let me make it a little more personal: Tell me, 'George,' do you love Jesus?"

The man was beside himself. The very idea, the affront of the question. How dare anyone ask about such a personal and potentially emotional topic? Why, that was between him and Jesus.

The point, of course, is that our love for Jesus needs to be immediate, intense, and quite often overwhelming. A deeply personal love, yes, but also a love that is profoundly visible. If we do not allow ourselves to fall in love with the Savior to the extent that our emotions, our thoughts, and ultimately our behaviors are all touched and enlarged by that love—then our spiritual journey will not take us much farther than tentative participation at best.

India? I don't know about India. But a love like that certainly will take us somewhere.

Love for Jesus changes us from the inside out.

10   JESUS' PRAYER AND OUR DECISION TO LOVE

I have given them your word, and the world has hated them because they do not belong to the world, just as I do not belong to the world.

—John 17:14

Whoever says, "I am in the light," while hating a brother or sister, is still in the darkness.

—1 John 2:9

It is critical that we understand Christ's perspective on the subject and the practice of love. Jesus never talked about Christian unity in any other context. Love stands in opposition to fear, and of course, the absence of love promotes disunity and division. "There is no fear in love, but perfect love casts out fear; for fear has to do with punishment, and whoever fears has not reached perfection in love. We love because he first loved us" (1 John 4:18-19).

A careful reading of John 17 reveals how deeply Jesus loved his disciples, and how completely he loves those of us who choose to follow him today. We can find this amazing and encouraging selection of scripture at the end of John's lengthy account that details Christ's Last Supper and sums up the essence of so much of his teaching.

Let's set the stage.

It has been several days since Jesus rode into Jerusalem on a donkey, an act carefully designed to signify his role as a king who comes triumphantly yet in peace. It has been quite a week. Luke's Gospel outlines some of the turmoil in chapters 19–21, such as the day Jesus turned over tables in the Temple and challenged the practice of "business as usual" in his Father's house. Just a few days earlier Jesus had publicly wept over the city of Jerusalem, and then he told a parable about wicked tenants who killed the landowner's son. Christ also referred to himself as the cornerstone, watched a poor widow make a profound gift, foretold the destruction of the Temple and Jerusalem, denounced the scribes, prayed every night, and preached every morning. The clock was winding down; Jesus knew exactly what was happening.

Finally, as the feast of Passover approached, Jesus told Peter and John to make arrangements to meet for one final dinner party together.

One unusual feature of this particular occasion was that Jesus already had a plan in place. The Master was not generally the detail guy for the operation. Christ typically took in the big picture, and throughout the four Gospels it is fairly clear that other people tended to take charge of logistics. This time, however, the Teacher himself had carefully set things up. "So they went and found everything as he had told them; and they prepared the Passover meal" (Luke 22:13).

John goes on to devote five chapters, a quarter of his entire manuscript, to sharing the story of that extraordinary meal. The words of Jesus speak through the centuries with a deep urgency and a focused passion. Jesus wants to make sure that his message is clear and that the path of spiritual formation he had already set in motion would continue on the right track.

They had spent three years together, learning day by day in their practical small-group experience. The Master and his disciples were committed to each other, and they had grown closer than brothers. Now, as their time together drew to a close, Jesus had some important ideas to get across. Are we really listening to his prayer?

An amazing prayer

At the end of the evening, as their meal together winds down and just before they go out to Gethsemane to pray, Jesus delivers this amazing prayer. First he prays for himself, then he prays for those disciples present around the table, and finally he prays for us. Jesus prays for me—Derek Maul; he prays for the men in my small group—Gary, Eric, Darrell, Gerard, Andy, Henry, Brad, and the others; and he prays for every one of us who claim to follow him today.

Wow! When you think about it, and especially considering the timing of this particular supplication, the sentiments communicated by the Son of God himself have got to be considered as more than a little weighty. The words of Christ are freighted with a level of gravitas we are compelled to heed.

Fact is, the way Jesus prayed for me and for you, with such ardor, with such deep affection and love, should say a lot about how we conduct ourselves as Christian men.

Let's take a look at some of the things the Savior touched on in his prayer in John 17:

1. "The words that you gave to me I have given to them, and they have received them and know in truth that I came from you" (v. 8).

Deliberate and prayerful consideration of the Bible is foundational to our life together as followers of Jesus. God's words not only form us, but they shape our character too.

One of the guys in my group was concerned about the absence of Christlike grace he tended to exhibit on his drive to work, then later at home after his drive back. Plus he was upset at himself for "acting like a jerk half the time in the office." He argued that God should take the initiative and change him more noticeably.

"With or without your active participation?" I asked for clarification.

"That's the point," he responded. "Shouldn't God be making it easier for me?"

He was serious. That's one of the great things about my friends; they don't make stuff up just to sound like they're all jazzed-up Christians and on the ball when really, like most of us the majority of the time, they're not.

"Tell us about your drive to work," I asked.

"Well, I usually listen to the news or talk radio," he said. "Sometimes I'm running late, so I drive hard and yell at the other commuters. I use a lot of hand signals."

"How about when you get to the office?"

"Stuff's piled up, so I dive right in. No one ever cleans the coffee pot, so I'm usually out of luck and ticked off at how selfish everyone else is. Things usually go downhill from there."

But didn't Jesus say that he had given us God's own words, and that he shared the truth of them with us?

After we read verse 8 again (we usually revisit verses from the focal scripture passage during our discussion), one of the guys—Darrell—

told how he has learned to turn off angry radio and instead has started listening to the Christian music station. Sometimes, he said, he spends some of the drive time in prayer—eyes open, of course!

Bob talked about the way he works hard to stay connected to the truth. Every day, no matter what urgency is sitting on his desk waiting to pounce on him when he arrives at the office, he reads a few verses of scripture and pauses to spend a few minutes in prayer. "Rather than wasting valuable company time," he said, "it turns out that I'm sharper and more productive the days I start off that way."

Another man talked about leaving home a little earlier to take the pressure off the drive and then using his occasional early arrival to clear the day with God before ever leaving his car.

"I remember the coffee pot problem from when I was a teacher," I added. "God challenged me to quit complaining and start following Christ. He made me rethink the situation so much that I brought in a new coffee pot to share. I started to clean it myself when other people left it dirty, and I often served my colleagues simply as an act of unconditional love."

2. "All mine are yours, and yours are mine; and I have been glorified in them" (v. 10).

Question: How was Jesus glorified? Answer: The Bible is pretty clear that Jesus was glorified through service, sacrificial love, and eventual death on the cross.

In Philippians 2:5-9 Paul said that Jesus "emptied himself, taking the form of a slave." He reminded Christians that Jesus "humbled himself and became obedient to the point of death. . . . Therefore God also highly exalted him." Paul suggests that we ought to have the same mind, attitude, and disposition as Christ.

I can't help but think of all the people who use the Christian faith to control, to put others down, and to promote their own interests/agendas/selves; who routinely fight and argue with other believers; and who jostle for status, power, prestige, and position.

Jesus is glorified in us inasmuch as we imitate his self-sacrificial love. If we want to grow spiritually, our lives must be all about dying to self, sacrificing self for our brothers and sisters, emptying ourselves, and taking the form of servants.

That is how the world will know that we belong to Jesus.

That is how Jesus is glorified in us. But it's certainly not easy.

I'll concede that following Christ in the Way is not easy—and especially not for men raised in a culture that glorifies personal achievement, personal gain, and prestige measured in respect to domination of others. But it was not easy for Jesus either. Jesus asked that—if it were possible—the cup the Father had offered him might pass. Jesus literally lost drops of blood through his sweat in the garden. Jesus listened to people malign him, make up all manner of lies about him, and call for his death.

Jesus did not say, "Follow me and I'll magically make my way convenient and profitable so you can look like successful guys to all your friends and thereby not lose face."

No, Jesus said this: "If any want to become my followers, let them deny themselves and take up their cross daily and follow me. For those who want to save their life will lose it, and those who lose their life for my sake will save it. What does it profit them if they gain the whole world, but lose or forfeit themselves?" (Luke 9:23-25).

3. "Holy Father, protect them in your name that you have given me, so that they may be one, as we are one" (v. 11).

This is not the first time that Jesus refers to unity as a means of identifying his friends. Twelve guys; or, thanks to Judas, down to eleven by this stage of the evening. Jesus already recognized in his companions the possibility of division. Yet at the same time he also sensed the powerful potential for unity, for dynamic agreement in love. Jesus knew that unity, that love, would be the most critical element of discipleship and especially of public witness—if the mission he had in mind for them was to have even the vaguest possibility of a snowball's chance.

So here we are, somewhere around two thousand years down the road. I can't help but wonder how Jesus thinks about where we stand today. Not so good regarding unity; not so good when it comes to Christ's desire that we are "one in his name."

My prayer is that a wide range of people from a broad variety of church backgrounds read this text. I pray that each one of you is asking God to lead you into a more authentic Christian witness. And I pray—along with Jesus—that we all will be one.

Let me tell you what I think about denominations. Denominations are a good thing. I truly believe that having different flavors of church is a wonderful idea because we have so many different flavors of people. People are unique, and we are all wired differently; that's the beauty of individuality. Indeed, God created us this way. Consequently there are varieties of experience in worship that are appropriate for every possible variation of Christian disciple.

"Mike" pastors a lively independent charismatic community church in the Florida panhandle. Once a month he meets with a small interdenominational ministers' support group, along with a Presbyterian, a Baptist, an Episcopalian, a United Methodist, and a Lutheran.

During one meeting Mike confided to his friends, "It's a good thing we have a variety of churches where people can worship. The straightlaced folk need a place to go; the people who enjoy liturgy need somewhere comfortable for them; some of you are just right for parishioners who don't like to get their feathers ruffled; and of course the Methodists are perfect if you enjoy a good potluck supper once a week."

His eyes were twinkling, so the others knew he wasn't done.

The Presbyterian minister finally bit. "So what kinds of people are attracted to your church, Mike?"

"That's easy," he laughed. "There has to be somewhere for all the crazies to go!"

I mentioned before that I have written well over one hundred feature stories about Christian ministers. Without exception I have enjoyed fellowship with these pastors as my brothers and sisters in Christ. Ministers of traditional downtown Methodist congregations; uptown Catholic priests; all sorts of Presbyterians; a Pentecostal Holiness pastor; senior pastors of several suburban Baptist megachurches; Lutherans, both Missouri Synod and Evangelical; Episcopalians; Assemblies of God; Independents; Primitive Baptists; and a Foursquare church. Caucasian, African American, Hispanic, Asian; high church, low church; old, young; men, women. From the Russian Orthodox priest who wore elaborate vestments and a huge hat for his interview to the plainspoken farmer who also shepherds a small interdenominational flock on weekends.

What we all have in common is Jesus. That's what the Lord was praying about in John 17, although sadly the concept still eludes far too many people who claim to be followers of his word. "Little children, let us love, not in word or speech, but in truth and action. And by this we will know that we are from the truth and will reassure our hearts before him" (1 John 3:18-19).

Why have the ways of Jesus made such a small foothold in the world after twenty centuries of effort? Really, it's not like the church is all that much closer to winning over the planet than we were, say, five hundred years ago. I am convinced that the answer was anticipated in Christ's prayer and that he knew what was at stake when he said that he longed for his followers to be one. We are not about to win the world for Christ when we condemn those who vary from our narrow viewpoint, rant about what we are against more than who we are for, and fight among ourselves over every variation of doctrine. People must know we are Christians because our love for one another is so evident—Jesus said that! In the context of such unity, I believe, anything becomes possible.

4. "I speak these things in the world so that they may have my joy made complete in themselves. I have given them your word, and the world has hated them because they do not belong to the world, just as I do not belong to the world" (vv. 13-14).

Jesus has spoken this prayer so that each of us may know the completeness of joy. But we need to be clear about joy. Jesus is not talking about joy as in, "Yahoo, I just won a million dollars!"

Jesus is not interested in lucrative business deals, overflowing bank accounts, or creating idyllic scenarios where our lives will be easy and trouble-free. Indeed, any "gospel" that promises prosperity or convenience as a sign of divine blessing misses the point of Christ's teaching. Christ is most definitely interested, however, in our experiencing genuine joy—the joy of our salvation, the joy of living in his most excellent way.

We are called to live as forgiven people, overflowing with authentic joy and living in the unity of the Spirit.

What I mean to say, Jesus points out, is that my followers no longer belong to the world. Christ's kind of living—kingdom living—is seriously countercultural. Christ's way is countercultural as regards a consumer society that both expects sacrifice and offers reward at the altars of commerce. And his kingdom is also countercultural regarding our "We're right; you're wrong" brands of religiosity, the narrow-minded games that have little room for a Jesus who speaks with such compassion and such inclusiveness through the Gospels.

5. "Sanctify them in the truth; your word is truth" (vv. 16-17).

When Pontius Pilate asked Jesus the famous question, "What is truth?" he was posing a question that begged an answer he was not spiritually equipped to understand. Pilate teaches us that we cannot use the standards and measurements of this world to prove or to disprove the Christian faith.

This idea can be especially problematic for men. We like to prove ourselves in the arenas where we live. We like to play and we like to win. If the particular arena where we are being tested is this world, it is hard for us to give up the pursuit of success—even when the values we aspire to stand in direct contradiction to the gospel.

Again we need to look to Jesus as our example and guide. Jesus was humble and meek; he remained passive when attacked; he preached a message of reconciliation; and he rode into Jerusalem on a donkey. Jesus led by serving; he ministered to the needs of others as his constant priority; he said that we should love our enemies; and he washed the disciples' dirty feet. Jesus focused his energy on building God's kingdom, not some temporary edifice. He gave away everything he had rather than accumulating lots of stuff. He did not consider financial gain a viable measure of success on any level, unless it was the achievement of using those resources to help our brothers and sisters. Why? Because we understand the resources never really were ours to begin with except to hold in trust for God.

6. "I ask not only on behalf of these, but also on behalf of those who will believe in me through their word, that they may all be one" (vv. 20-21).

That would be me, that would be you, and that would be every other person who accepts the pointed message Christ delivers with such faithfulness and such positive energy. Jesus is our personal advocate; he was thinking specifically about us and our individual situations when he poured out his heart to the Father. It is the deep desire of our Savior to see us in fellowship with other Christians. If we believe him and say that we love him, what could possibly stand in our way?

Why does this mean so much to Jesus? "So that the world may know that you have sent me and have loved them even as you have loved me" (v. 23). Jesus is looking for evidence that we are doing a little more than merely paying lip service to his startling sacrifice on the cross. Jesus is not one to equivocate. Regarding something this important, neither should we.

Trust

> Surely I know the plans I have for you, says the LORD, plans for your welfare and not for harm, to give you a future with hope. Then when you call upon me and come and pray to me, I will hear you. When you search for me, you will find me; if you seek me with all your heart, I will let you find me, says the LORD, and I will restore your fortunes and gather you from all the nations and all the places where I have driven you, says the LORD, and I will bring you back to the place from which I sent you into exile. (Jer. 29:11-14)

Exile is a dark place, a place that values just about everything that opposes the truth of the gospel of Jesus. My exile is all about me; it demands financial prosperity, craves public recognition, wants to control other people, seeks to defeat those people with the temerity to oppose my will. In short, it seeks personal validation in the currency of the culture that has taught me so well.

When Jesus brings me back from exile in the way that Jeremiah prophesied, he builds confidently on a foundation of simple trust. Trust not in things but in the faithfulness and the abiding love of God in Christ Jesus.

Trust is the foundation of my faith. To be honest, I'm not sure that most of us take the idea of trusting God seriously. Are we really in the place where we absolutely trust God in Jesus? I'd have to say no, at least not to the extent that Christ imagined when he prayed such a personal prayer at the end of the Last Supper, just before he headed out to the inevitability of betrayal, of abandonment, of torture, and of brutal death.

Trust fall

My friend Steve jumped out of an airplane; in fact, he used to do it all the time. A highly trained airborne soldier, Steve was fully confident that his parachute would open. He was also confident in his reserve.

So he leaned out the door, launched himself into thin air, and looked forward to experiencing the familiar rush of exhilaration followed by a gentle floating before safely reaching his final destination on terra firma.

Well, he reached the ground all right, but unfortunately he got there much sooner than expected. Neither of his two parachutes opened. "The main parachute blew out," he said, "then the reserve tangled in what was left of it."

Steve doesn't remember the exact details of the rapid fall; he only knows that he lived and that his recovery was lengthy. He vaguely remembers the medics pulling dirt out of his mouth as he drifted in and out of consciousness.

Steve did one more jump after his recovery to prove to himself that he could face his biggest fear. But since then, he doesn't jump out of airplanes anymore. I believe it has something to do with trust issues.

"From that point on, the permanence of life was not all that it's made out to be," Steve said. "Life is precious, yes, but it is also transient. It is neither the beginning nor the end of what really matters."

Steve does, however, trust in God. He trusts in Jesus Christ, and you have to respect that level of confidence from someone who went through what he did on the outer fringes of the realm the rest of us glibly like to call "a leap of faith."

Steve, of course, insists that his experience of God is no leap of faith at all. "Jumping out of an airplane with a parachute, even one you have packed yourself," he said, "and trusting that the darned thing's going to open—now that's a leap of faith. When I talk about Jesus, I'm talking about something a lot more solid and a good deal more reliable than that. God's faithfulness is from everlasting to everlasting."

I'm right there with Steve. When I say I trust God, it means that I trust God as I trust gravity (no joke, Steve knows exactly what I mean!). I trust in God the same way I trust that the sun will rise each morning, that the imperative of life will have its way in my garden, and that spring will absolutely follow winter. My faith is ironclad. That's what I mean when I say trust.

We don't reach that kind of trust outside of experience. And I don't mean through experiments or the little tests we give God to make ourselves feel better. I trust God because my belief is grounded today in year after year of real-world familiarity and know-how. I trust God because his faithfulness counts for something in my life.

In a nutshell, that's what it means to be a disciple. It means to soak ourselves in the God-experience so that, little by little, the Greatest Story Ever Told becomes our story. It became mine, or at least it is still becoming my story. And it's a story I have come to enjoy even more in the telling.

> There you will serve other gods made by human hands, objects of wood and stone that neither see, nor hear, nor eat, nor smell. From there you will seek the LORD your God, and you will find him if you search after him with all your heart and soul. In your distress, when all these things have happened to you in time to come, you will return to the LORD your God and heed him. Because the LORD your God is a merciful God, he will neither abandon you nor destroy you; he will not forget the covenant with your ancestors that he swore to them. (Deut. 4:28-31)

God will never forget the covenant he has made.

11   HONEST TO GOD

Learning to love by learning to receive love

God wants to know me, yet he will not impose himself on the relationship. God wants me to know him, yet he is never pushy.

It's not so much a matter of confessing our sins to God—he already knows our shortcomings. The power and the intimacy come in revealing layer after layer of our personal selves.

—Get Real, *pages 114–15*

The LORD searches every heart and understands every motive behind the thoughts. If you seek him, he will be found by you.

—*1 Chronicles 28:9,* NIV

I regard everything as loss because of the surpassing value of knowing Christ Jesus my Lord. For his sake I have suffered the loss of all things, and I regard them as rubbish, in order that I may gain Christ.

—*Philippians 3:8*

Probably the greatest impediment to my personal spiritual growth has been my inability to be honest with God. Closely related to, and inescapably tied up in, my spiritual honesty is my willingness—or reluctance—to be honest with myself. It is really amazing what you can keep from yourself if you work long and hard enough at the process.

The watershed experience in this particular aspect of my spiritual journey dates back to one fateful year somewhere in my midthirties. On the surface, matters in my household couldn't have looked better.

I was teacher of the year at my school and becoming respected throughout the county as an authority on emotionally disturbed children. My wife, Rebekah, was redefining ministry to young families at our church, finding her unique voice, and becoming a regional keynote speaker in growing demand. Our days were amazing, breathtaking, spectacular even—yet extremely complex and thorny at the same time. In many ways life was wonderful, but it was exceedingly difficult too.

Our children were around nine and eleven at the time, so the middle grades and those challenging teenage years were coming up, right on the horizon. Occasionally, things at school did not go so well; at home, tension subtly began to mount. Slowly, little by little, my confidence started to unravel.

Enter "exhibit A," stage left. Imagine, if you can enlarge your willful suspension of disbelief to accommodate such a thought, a young father and husband of ten years with maybe the tad of a possible tendency toward—and you know this has to be entirely hypothetical if it involves me—denial.

OK, I know it's a stretch to even contemplate any American man, especially me, experiencing any level of denial! But I have to admit my bottom-line approach to inconvenience, challenge, heartache, and all manner of problems in my life has always been to simply close my eyes and hope it will all go away.

And my experience taught me that denial works a great deal of the time. Things did go away, even if only just a little way under the surface. Plus my record regarding intervention was not exactly stellar at that stage of my career as a man. Given the proven risk-reward theory, and with my fumbling around trying to fix things pretty much guaranteed to make everything worse, closing my eyes and wishing problems to simply go away seemed to make a lot of practical sense.

I was also fairly well practiced in the fine art of putting things off till later; I was a big fat procrastinator. Even then, however, I eventually came to understand that I was really just as likely to make-believe that such and such a problem, challenge, or roadblock did not even exist. Things weren't so much put off as they were put away.

The term I have coined for this malady is MPD (Male Pattern Denial).

If, as we have already discussed in this book, honest desire for God is such a critical ingredient for any significant path of spiritual formation, then we are going to have to acknowledge our need for God's grace in the first place. But the scope of our need was too hard for me to face, so I pushed it all aside and simply prayed that the problems would go away.

Love predicated on knowledge needs something to feed the flame

My wife has a favorite saying about our relationship. "The most wonderful thing about Derek," she often tells people, "is that he knows me and yet he loves me anyway."

She has always been authentic, genuine, bona fide. I never once had the impression, even in our early dating, that Rebekah presented any sort of facade. "What you see is what you get" has always been a critical component of my wife's personal credo, and it has served her well in everything she does.

She tells stories about some of the other girls in her dormitory when we attended Stetson University together. Her friends sometimes kept a date waiting in the lobby an hour or longer while they made sure that hair, makeup, apparel, perfume, shoes, and every conceivable item on their extensive predate checklist was just so. She insisted she knew several women who actually got married having never allowed the young man in their lives to see anything other than the fully loaded, finely tuned, fanatically detailed version of their carefully applied persona. Obviously spontaneity had no place in these relationships.

I remember stopping by her dorm early one morning to meet for a preclass breakfast off campus. Rebekah sported jeans, flip-flops, a flannel shirt, and a bandanna over her head because she had no time for a shampoo. Her roommate was horrified. I thought she was gorgeous.

Our first Valentine's Day Rebekah planned to share a boatload of truth with me that she was convinced would likely end the relationship. Instead I made her a cup of tea and listened. When she was through, I loved her even more.

Yet, inexplicably, I fell into the pattern of not affording her the same investment in authenticity and trust.

By the time our midthirties rolled around, my wife realized there was an inequity between us that was becoming harder and harder to bridge. She realized, sadly, that she did not know me very well. Such loss of confidence and trust will stifle any relationship, and eventually it did ours.

We treat God the same way

Any forward motion in our communion with God relies on a set of similar dynamics. God knows us and—amazingly—loves us anyway.

But if we do not care to know God, or if we do not care to reveal our-selves in any meaningful way to God, then the relationship is going to slow to a crawl before eventually dying on the vine.

Here's what is so profound about that watershed year in my mid-thirties. My relationship with my wife paralleled my relationship to God. A fix for one would amount to a fix for both.

My wife, it turns out, is pushier than God and way less subtle. So the fix was initiated when she put out a simple ultimatum: "Either we learn how to communicate with the help of a professional, or I'm going to have to believe that you are not at all interested in saving this marriage."

What I realized—in fairly short order—was that my failure to be hon-est with my wife really meant that I was not being honest with myself.

Indeed, that's why I had been resistant at first regarding the notion that I had anything at all to do with the broken relationship. I didn't "get it." Consider the following:

1. How could I be accused of holding back—I reasoned—if there was nothing that I was consciously keeping inside?
2. I truly believed that I was being both genuine and honest.
3. Unfortunately, all I was giving my wife was the extent of everything I was willing to reveal to myself. Even if that was everything I had on hand, it simply wasn't enough for either of us or for God.

We tend to build barriers to growth in our relationships out of a misplaced sense of self-preservation. If I can't handle the fact that my hopes and dreams are all confused and that I don't know what I'm doing as a parent, then I will doubtless believe that my wife can't han-dle it either. So of course I clammed up.

Instead of allowing my wife to help me, I was driving her away. I didn't trust Rebekah enough to let her know my inadequacies (I didn't consciously think that, but it was obviously the case), so I rejected her by closing off the most intimate soul knowledge that is—quite liter-ally—the heart and the hope of great relationships.

God loves me that way

God loves me that way too. Instead of allowing God to know me, I was keeping God at a distance. God wants to know me, yet he will not impose himself on the relationship. God wants me to know him, yet he is never pushy.

It's not so much a matter of confessing our sins to God—he already knows our shortcomings. The power and the intimacy come in revealing layer after layer of our personal selves. Hopes, dreams, fears, failures, what we think about absolutely every issue under the sun and what we think—this is critical—about the people we love.

Do we love God that way?

Loving God that way necessarily involves a lot of listening. It involves a lot of study: "Have you read my book?" And it involves a lot of prayer. Maybe we have taken a step toward letting God know us more completely. If so, good. But have you ever been on a date where only one person learned about the other? It is critical to give God the same quality of attention we demand of him.

But let me share a secret. The more we invest our time and attention in getting to know God, the easier it is for us to love God. Remember what was happening with my wife? I might have been falling more deeply in love with her, but in holding out on self-revelation, I was effectively cutting off the fuel for her love for me.

Answers

Let me share a little more about what happened. First, we got help. We talked with a counselor who also knew and loved God. We planned our sessions like dates, every week for quite a long time. At 4:30 we went to the counselor's office, where we spent one hour in pretty intense stuff designed to facilitate mutual knowing. Then at 6:00 we had dinner out so we could review the session, talk about our homework, and begin to explore the new margins of our life together.

Listen, guys, I understand completely that this stuff is not easy. We build incredibly resistant barriers to authentic love in our hearts and minds. Some of these barricades are cultural, some genetic, and some are all-natural, 100-percent "man"—meaning that probably 90 percent of males in the entire world will clam up in certain ways because of some embedded fight-or-flee reflex that might have saved us at some time from the wrath of the saber-toothed tiger but nowadays just helps to screw up our relationships and get us in trouble with our wives.

Whatever. We still have to deal with stuff, so deal with it we did.

There I was, sitting on a small couch with my wife and across from Dr. D., beginning to understand that the more I allow myself to be loved, the more capable I become of Christlike love in my own heart.

Rather than my inadequacies and shortcomings exposing me for the sham I believed I was and releasing the rejection I knew I deserved, such self-disclosure and honest desire for positive change opened the floodgates of deeper affection and unbounded acceptance. I'm imperfect—embrace me; I know I can be a real jerk—give me a hug; yes, I'm a needy, self-centered ass—let the lovefest begin!

I'm not being cynical here. The dynamics of authentic relationship are just that topsy-turvy when examined in the light of the ambient culture. For years we have learned that "real men" should avoid vulnerability, stiff-arm self-revelation, refrain from disclosing our true feelings, and play it cool at all costs because we need to be strong.

Fact: We will never move forward in our relationship with God until we have the strength and resolve to bring every aspect of our most honest selves to the cross.

Fact: We will never love God with much more than the surface of our hearts until we allow God to love a lot more than the surface of who we really are.

Fact: God will not reject us when we come clean about the unsavory contents of our hearts and minds.

Fact: If we continue to insist on keeping God's unconditional and all-encompassing love at arm's length, most likely we will reject God, perhaps for a long time.

Fact: When Jesus wrestled in prayer in the garden just before he gave himself over to humiliation, torture, and death, he faced far worse than the dark recesses of our murky souls. Once we choose to embrace the full extent of his love, we will be better able to love him in return.

Warning: This is dangerous stuff. One reason I held back for so long in my relationship as a husband to Rebekah was a thinly veiled fear—perfectly legitimate, it turns out—that my life would never be the same. So, if you want your life to remain the same, if being mired in mediocrity and surface-level love is your idea of a great rest of your life, then by all means close the book now.

However, if you dare to live, tear down the veil and take Jesus at his word. Allow him to love all of you and then love him back. I swear your life will never be the same.

DARING

12 WHAT DO WE DARE?

Take up the whole armor of God, so that you may be able to withstand on that evil day, and having done everything, to stand firm.

—*Ephesians 6:13*

In the world you face persecution. But take courage; I have conquered the world!

—*John 16:33*

In the story of *Braveheart,* Scottish national hero William Wallace declares, "Every man dies; not every man really lives."

Wallace was well aware of the difference between merely existing—something he witnessed in too many men who failed to respond to the challenge of a full and engaging life—and the wonder of actually living to their full potential. Mediocrity is a sad curse that threatens to suck the lifeblood from many people, people who might otherwise pursue lives that actually mean something beyond the day in, day out of survival.

We all know people who constantly regress to the unremarkable. We may sometimes be tempted to follow that path ourselves. It is too easy to fall into patterns of below average, develop a comfortable rhythm there, and consequently live out our lives without ever pushing any kind of envelope at all.

One missionary who worked in the island nation of Haiti for many years put his finger on the distinction between life and the sad absence of significance. He was talking with a visiting pastor about his agricultural school and vocational training ministry. "You are doing a great work by helping the people survive in these difficult circumstances," she observed.

"Survive?" the missionary responded with a wry smile. "Why, it doesn't take anything to survive. The challenge of the gospel is to teach people how to thrive!"

Jesus' ministry was—and is—all about the difference between scraping out an existence and living in the fullness that is always God's intention. "I came that they may have life," Jesus said, "and have it abundantly" (John 10:10).

Like William Wallace, Jesus understood on a fundamental level that life at full tilt is not necessarily safe, never lackluster, and certainly not anywhere close to easy. Life lived on the level of abundance, so far as Jesus is concerned, was never considered optional—is never considered optional. "Whoever does not carry the cross and follow me cannot be my disciple" (Luke 14:27).

To be a Christian man in the twenty-first century is—essentially—to be countercultural. Faith-filled living always involves standing out as somewhat different from the run-of-the-mill. That is a large part of what Christ means by "carrying the cross"; that's what it means to really live. It is—usually—surprisingly easy to follow the crowd, and once we fall into that pattern, it becomes astonishingly hard to buck the system. To be honest, I have to admit that following Jesus in this way turns out to be one of my biggest personal challenges, because for me the greatest and most deadly temptation has always been that of the easy, carefree life.

Roll out the easy chair

The easy chair is my icon of temptation. Let me explain. Take any group of a dozen faithful disciples. If each man in turn were to share a symbol that represented temptation in his life, there would be a lot to choose from. One may say money: "I want it so bad, sometimes the wanting drives me." Another would share his need for drink: "I'm dry; I'm recovering, but the bottle is my number one temptation." The list would go on: gambling, success, video games, pornography, more—of anything he has, avoidance, denial, food, power, control—probably something different for every man. For me, the temptation is and always has been "the easy road."

Simply put, if I'm not careful, I can be lazy in a heartbeat. Give me a nice leather chair, a good book, and a mug of hot coffee. That's all I need. If a challenge comes along, I'd rather not know about it. Don't bother me; I'm sure it will pass. I'm comfortable, you know.

And there it is—my biggest temptation.

Jesus disturbs all that

Jesus disturbs all that and more. God's plan for our lives is for us to be the best we can possibly be and to serve him with 100 percent of the gifts he has given us, nothing less. This is one reason, I believe, that God ordered the circumstances of my life to force some major changes early on. God wanted me to become all that my unique creation made possible, and one way God got me jump-started was by sending me to America. Not that I couldn't have moved forward in England; it's just that God needed to move me out of my comfort zone, and he had just the people lined up over here to make that happen.

I had things a little too easy growing up. I had plenty of natural abilities, a good mind, and a loving family within which to grow. In sports I was unusually well coordinated, and it was easy to be the best at every game I ever tried. But I was never the very best I could have been—because for me it was enough just to be good. I ran a 10.1-second hundred yards, for example, but never learned how to use starting blocks and never worked out. I jumped over twenty feet in the long jump, but I never practiced, and the twelve jumps I did in four meets were the only ones I ever tried. I was one of the best soccer players in southeast England but limited my practice to warm-ups before games.

Eventually I tripped up. Academically, coasting by on natural ability is not an option. I failed successively as a teen, wasting years of potential while attending one of the premier preparatory schools in all of England. So I flunked my way through high school and was, of course, rejected by all the colleges I approached. My first job out of school found a fairly intelligent brain stuffing baskets of soggy towels and sheets into giant-sized dryers at an industrial laundry. I rode a battered one-speed bike five miles to work, earned the equivalent of thirty-six dollars a week, and wondered what my life would become.

Then the great and mysterious designs of providence brought me somehow to America (it's a long story). One early September found "Mr. Relaxed" at the tired end of his first week of presoccer season two-a-days at Stetson University in central Florida. Stetson is the kind of school where relaxation is not an option, and excellence is not merely a virtue—it is expected to be a reflex.

And so for the first time in my life, I had to really push myself. The combination of heat, fatigue, and a little genuine effort led to the inevitable: I threw up. At this point, leaning over the fence, I got my first real understanding of how Americans view sports. Instead of the sympathy I expected, and maybe a cup of water, or the coach suggesting I sit out for a few minutes, all I heard was: "Yeah!" "All right!" "Right on!" "Way to go, my man!" and "Hey, look at that, the Limey threw up!" One of the players even said, with all seriousness, "Aw rats, I wanted to be the first."

I gradually began to understand that losing my lunch at a workout was considered a virtue and that, quite by accident, I had proven myself.

I even picked up this spirit in class and—during my four years at the university—moved from straight C's my first semester to finish up with mostly A's my senior year. And it gave me great satisfaction, several years later, to let my old high school teachers in England know that I had become one of them, entering teaching after my second degree, focused and doing my absolute best in school, summa cum laude.

Excellence and the bread of life

That's what God wants from us: our best. He doesn't just want it for himself, God wants it for us. For the Christ-follower, excellence in all things is the essential substance of a life well lived.

"Jesus said to them, 'I am the bread of life. Whoever comes to me will never be hungry, and whoever believes in me will never be thirsty'" (John 6:35).

Bread is code for the substance of life. When Jesus talked about the core material of our being, the essence of what life is all about when it comes down to the basics, he was talking about being and doing whatever it is that God has called us to do or equipped us to be. "He said to them, 'I have food to eat that you do not know about.' So the disciples said to one another, 'Surely no one has brought him something to eat?' Jesus said to them, 'My food is to do the will of him who sent me and to complete his work'" (John 4:32-34).

Doing God's will is the action part of this Christianity equation. It is what happens when we get up the gumption to own and to step out into the marvelous truth and the inspiring promise that have the potential to define our lives as followers of Jesus.

We have talked about the desire each one of us owns to know God and to embrace the redemption and the fullness of life that are bound up in being a Jesus-follower. Next we considered the decision to become a disciple, the deliberateness and the practice of learning and of putting ourselves in the right setting to grow. Then there is devotion, the wonder of our falling for God—heart, mind, and soul. This is the love that leads directly to action. Action is the imperative that completes the picture and feeds our growth as people of faith.

Faith is necessarily an action word

Mike was a member of my Men's Room for just a short while before his family moved away. He taught all of us a powerful lesson in daring, the butterflies-in-the-stomach kind of courage that involves engaging the message of Christ with immediacy and action. Mike's story demonstrates just what can happen when we are willing to say with all honesty, "Teach me your way, O LORD, that I may walk in your truth; give me an undivided heart to revere your name" (Ps. 86:11). Mike walked in God's truth.

As a group we had been talking about the disciple Peter's experience when he walked on the water. Peter jumped out of the safety of his fishing boat and joined Jesus right there on top of the less-than-calm surface of the Sea of Galilee. We were especially impressed that Peter had the guts to actually climb out of the bobbing craft while the other eleven more tentative followers grabbed on to the side of their comfort zone, holding on for dear life.

Another scripture passage, John 5:1-14, helped us with that particular study and speaks volumes about the same concept. It's another great story.

Jesus was in Jerusalem, and he made his way to the pool of Bethesda. It was, by all accounts, a beautiful place. There was a courtyard, colonnades, a pool of reputedly healing waters, and a crowd of would-be miracle recipients who relaxed all day waiting for something to happen. Friends and relatives took care of people who would otherwise be begging in the streets. Jesus walked right in and upset the status quo for a man who had been whining about his miserable situation for literally decades. Unfortunately, however, the man was not exactly ready for constructive change in his life, and he seemed to lack the will to actually get out of his comfortable boat and into the water.

John picks up the narrative: "One who was there had been an invalid for thirty-eight years. When Jesus saw him lying there and learned that he had been in this condition for a long time, he asked him, 'Do you want to get well?' 'Sir,' the invalid replied, 'I have no one to help me into the pool when the water is stirred. While I am trying to get in, someone else goes down ahead of me'" (John 5:5-7, NIV).

Even so, Jesus does not take action to cure the sick man until the "invalid" is willing to actually step out in faith and do something first. Absent of an action-based response from "Mr. Comfortable," the Healer knew that even a miracle of God never would have taken. In verse 8 Jesus commanded, "Get up! Pick up your mat and walk."

Talk in our Men's Room group had been centered around making a deliberate decision to respond to the challenge to risk walking on the water. The challenge in front of us was this: to get out of our boat, to pick up our mat, and to actually take those first tentative steps.

Mike was in a bind at work, and he knew it was time to move on. Unfortunately, the job market in his field was tight at the time, and he ran into a series of dead ends. One potential job, however, looked to be an exact fit. Problem was, management at the company could not make up their minds.

After a series of excellent interviews and some well-researched presentations, it all came down to Mike and one other man. At the last minute, however, management decided to kick the decision upstairs. It was announced that each candidate would have a winner-take-all five-minute interview with the big boss from corporate headquarters the following Monday morning, by phone. Neither man had ever met the CEO; his office was over one thousand miles away, and Mike saw his future slipping into the realm of chance.

Mike was beside himself. He had invested hours of time and effort cultivating a strong relationship with local management. He was convinced he had the right qualifications, and he was sure God wanted him to get this particular position, but all the effort was about to be for naught. The corporate CEO had no firsthand knowledge of the process, and five minutes cold turkey would be a lottery at best. Depressed and miserable, Mike went home for the weekend to pout.

Saturday afternoon, mowing the grass, Mike finally let God speak to his heart regarding the process. He asked God, "Teach me your way, O LORD, that I may walk in your truth." Suddenly it was clear as a bell. Action. Daring. "Pick up your mat and walk." God's way, more often than not, calls at some point for getting out of the boat.

Mike parked the lawn mower, walked into the house, immediately got on the phone, and purchased a round-trip airplane ticket. The next day, after church, he hopped onto the plane and flew to Maryland. There he rented a car and drove to the town where his potential new employer housed its corporate offices, and then he checked into a motel nearby. On Monday morning he pulled into the parking lot at 8:30 and dialed the number.

The executive assistant took the call. "Sir, he's scheduled to talk with you later; I'll be back in touch with you at 9:30. It's not a good idea to interrupt him before then."

"I'd appreciate it if you'd let me talk to him now."

"Believe me, sir, you don't want to do that."

"I'll take the risk."

So Mike was patched through. The corporate director was not pleased. "What's this all about? I'm not scheduled to take your call for another hour."

"I'm in Maryland. I'd like to meet you," Mike said. "I'm standing outside the lobby door."

Silence.

"All I want is the opportunity to meet with you face-to-face."

The CEO relented, barely. "I guess we can do the interview in my office as well as on the phone," he said. "But I'm still not giving you any more than the five minutes."

"Fair enough," Mike said. He went on in.

I need to interject here that Mike had already spent a good deal of time in prayer over the previous thirty-six hours. He really was walking by faith and not by sight. He had started his morning on his knees; he had talked with God out in the parking lot; and he prayed his way up the elevator too.

When they met, the executive continued to be brusque and curt. He looked at his watch. "You have exactly five minutes," he growled. "Actually four; we've already used one. The clock's ticking."

"Thank you. Let me tell you why I'm here today," Mike began. "My men's Bible study group has been reading this book by John Ortberg called *If You Want to Walk on Water, You've Got to Get Out of the Boat.*"[1]

Mike looked the man directly in the eye. "I decided it was time to get out of the boat."

"Is that so?" the CEO replied, his face softening a tad. "Well, let me tell you about this wonderful book we've been studying at my church." The executive gestured toward a well-worn paperback on the front edge of his desk.

An hour later, while the two were still deep in conversation, the phone on the CEO's desk rang. "It's your 9:40 interview," the assistant said. Mike squirmed as he listened to his new boss curtly dismiss the other candidate in a little less than thirty seconds.

"Welcome aboard," the CEO said to Mike, and extended his hand.

13   LiViNG AS iF FAiTH ACTUALLY MAKES A DiFFERENCE

Only, live your life in a manner worthy of the gospel of Christ, so that, whether I come and see you or am absent and hear about you, I will know that you are standing firm in one spirit, striving side by side with one mind for the faith of the gospel, and are in no way intimidated by your opponents.

—*Philippians 1:27-28*

I'm going to crawl out on a limb here and suggest that one of our most troubling shortcomings as Christians is a lack of authenticity—the public presentation of a kind of feigned spirituality. We seem to be reluctant to let go of the props that help our faith fit in tidily with the ambient culture, so our experience—or at least our presentation—sometimes lacks the genuineness of unretouched truth. This all happens largely, I believe, because we are afraid of what too much "untreated raw Jesus" might do to upset our carefully crafted lives.

Why is it so hard to be open and honest about our love for God? Why do we struggle with being real about our doubts, our fears, our brokenness, and our missteps? Why are we reluctant to allow genuine faith to seep into our emotions and our work? Is it that hard to invite the people we say we love and care about into the truth and the discovery of our convictions, to be our companions in an honest exploration of what it means to love and to follow Jesus?

Too much of the public face of Christianity looks a lot like those tourists I read about in modern-day Israel who pretend to walk on the water at the Sea of Galilee. No, I'm not making this up. For just a few bucks, I understand, visitors to the area can make their way across a series of near-invisible Plexiglas pillars positioned as stepping-stones just beneath the water's surface. If they pay a little more, the fortunate pilgrims can take home a video of the sublime experience.

All of the razzmatazz, all the surface-level appearance of a divine encounter, but absent the deep cost and life-shaking conviction that defined the experience of someone like Peter.

Contrast edited and spliced video footage of happy tourists with the raw image of Peter plunging from the fishing boat in the middle of a stormy sea, completely immersing himself in Jesus. Imagine the faith life and the character of the early church had Peter merely tiptoed across Plexiglas stepping-stones on a calm day before hopping ashore to pick up his certificate of completion.

It's a sad and plastic image, isn't it? But it is also a chillingly relevant picture when we consider the presentation of Christianity in so many settings today. I know I often fail to jump in like Peter, and I doubt that someone with the moxie of the Galilean fisherman would even recognize the all-too-sanitized version of the Savior we try to palm off to the world we live in so much of the time.

As a schoolteacher I must have read C. S. Lewis's Chronicles of Narnia to my students a dozen times. Lewis's description of Aslan, the Christ figure in the story, is that of a savior who invites his followers to operate far outside of their comfort zone; he is at once both wild and good.

In the first book, *The Lion, the Witch and the Wardrobe,* the children ask their friends Mr. and Mrs. Beaver if Aslan is safe. "Who said anything about safe?" said Mr. Beaver. "'Course he isn't safe. But he's good. He's the King, I tell you."[1]

If we are only interested in a religion that is safe, then I don't recommend Christianity. But if we are up for something more, then we must engage a truth C. S. Lewis could not explain simply by way of intellectual argument and that we cannot dress up in Sunday clothes to then leave conveniently at the church.

At the Passover feast, Peter was reluctant to let Jesus wash his feet. "'No,' said Peter, 'you shall never wash my feet.' Jesus answered, 'Unless I wash you, you have no part with me.' 'Then, Lord,' Simon Peter replied, 'not just my feet but my hands and my head as well!'" (John 13:8-9, NIV).

Sometimes I suspect that Jesus embarrasses us, especially in front of our unchurched friends. "Just a little water," we say when he invites us in to swim. "I couldn't possibly go as far as you suggest. I have to consider my public image, you know."

No wonder we feel spiritually dry

The conversation was almost identical to a hundred others I have had in the past couple of years.

"I feel dry spiritually," "John" said. "Things are making sense in my mind, but I'm coming up empty when it comes to God's presence anywhere but at church. It's not so much that I doubt as that I'm not feeling my faith enough. It feels as if God is not there for me or really making any difference during the day. I seem to be able to go to work all week long without God ever coming into my heart or turning my spirit his way. I don't feel connected to God at all. And then I come back to church, and I realize how much I have missed God's presence."

"Let me make sure I'm understanding you correctly," I said. "You're feeling disappointed and a little left out because of your sense of isolation from God. It's as if God is absent most days."

"Pretty much every day," John said. "Especially at work; I just don't think about God at all."

John's dilemma is a constant question. How can we begin to consider being courageous witnesses to God's love through Christ when we have trouble even remembering that God exists when we leave the church or simply get into our car and drive to work?

Here's the scenario. We're busy; God's busy. We don't seem to get together much. Then the challenge is often exacerbated, I believe, by the tendency of many spiritually minded Christians to use "code" or super-spiritual language that suggests inaccurate or misleading information about the quality and the quantity of their spiritual experience.

We've all heard it. People who pepper their conversation with so many "Praise the Lord" references that you get the impression God rides around in the car with them all day—in the flesh, that Jesus takes them out to lunch, and that the Holy Spirit whispers spiritual encouragement in their ears during every facet of the day.

"I don't know how I would have pulled in those new accounts, praise God, if Jesus hadn't been leading me every step of the way."

"I just know that when I turned to the Lord—thank you, Jesus— God stopped my cold from turning into the flu."

"Praise the Lord, we were talking all morning, praise God, and I've felt his presence during every minute of the day this week."

"The Lord told me you were troubled, praise God, and he's placed a burden on my heart for your family."

After a few conversations like that, it's easy for the rest of us to come away feeling that we're missing out on something, that we are second-class or lower-tier believers, or that maybe somehow we got passed over when it comes to "real born-again faith."

Well, in fact Jesus does ride around in the car with them all the time. But we have to understand that Jesus rides around with us too. Jesus rides around with you, and Jesus rides around with me. The only difference is the important fact that the people with the religious "Jesus vocabulary" typically don't ignore the presence of the Savior like the rest of us. They either include the Lord in the details of their day-to-day lives with genuine and practiced attention, or they like to talk as if they do. Either way, there's something here for us to learn.

My friend's problem happens to be much less mysterious than his notion that he has been abandoned by God, or that he is missing out on a mystical experience that other people routinely enjoy. Fact is, God's Spirit doesn't come in a timed-release capsule or a patch that constantly emits a comforting signal all day long. And there is no hierarchy of religious experiences, as if crossing denominational lines, saying the right magic words, or getting baptized again or for the umpteenth time or by the right preacher will cause us to finally latch on to the "correct" formula, so we can at last find our place amongst God's "in crowd."

The people who talk as if their experience of God is a constant have simply made the decision to expand their spiritual consciousness in a more disciplined fashion.

Rather than fret that his connection with God is an afterthought much of the week, my friend John simply needs to develop a more proactive habit of talking with the Lord. One simple solution is to set a small hourly alarm and spend a short minute in prayer every time the thing beeps. It is no mystery to say that a week devoted to taking such deliberate steps would be a week John would look back on and recognize the presence of God in his life from hour to hour.

More than that, it would be a week where the presence of God began—subtly—to work into many aspects of John's life that he had never fully considered before. And that would just be the beginnings of where God wants him to be and what God wants him to dare.

Alive and well in the public schools

When I taught exceptional education in Florida's public schools, I designed a lot of creative exercises to bring my faith into the essential fabric of each day. I have already detailed how God used controlled breathing to help me ("The Long, Deep Breath," chap. 8). That simple practice did a lot to expand my working relationship with God.

Another effective intervention came during the first hour of each day in the classroom. Because I was one of those teachers who liked to be thoroughly prepared (all schoolteachers will affirm that surprises are seldom a good thing in the classroom), I usually arrived on site more than an hour early. When it was still very quiet—usually before I did anything else to get ready—I would sit at each student's desk and pray for him or her by name.

"Generous and loving Lord," I might pray, "please help me to be the tangible presence of Christ for Justin today. I ask that you help him as he struggles to control his temper; quiet his mind and touch his spirit. Speak through me, I pray. Amen."

Then I would move on, spending a minute at each place and lifting the student—and my teaching—before the throne of grace.

Let me tell you, and you can take this to the bank, it was impossible for me to exclude my faith from my work when I took the time to pray for my students. I usually went through my prayer routine three to four days per week, and the result—especially in terms of my having the strength and resolve to do my best—was ironclad.

The same principle will be just as effective for a sales representative before each call, for a manager outlining the priorities of the day, for a counselor organizing notes prior to a session, or for an administrator preparing for a meeting.

Bemoaning the observation that faith does not elbow its way into our daily stream of consciousness is a complete waste of time and effort. The remedy is in our hands; the practice is well within our capabilities; and the results are unarguably consistent.

How is this courageous?

At first, daring often amounts to little more than a simple response to our desire to know God more completely. We dare because we want to live more constant lives of faith.

Men like my friend John feel frustrated and disappointed about the sense of disconnect between their spiritual lives at church and their day-to-day experience as people inhabiting a secular world. The reason they are frustrated is that they want to expand their faith, and they feel stymied. Such frustration is a good sign.

If we are not familiar with wearing our Christian hat in the workplace, then any adjustment in that context—however small—can be understood as a heroic act of courage.

Another man, "Kevin," simply placed a small Bible on his desk. The sight of it reminded him to pray. He said he felt an instant and pervasive change in the way he went about his business. Later a colleague asked him what the Bible was doing out in public, and my friend shared this simple testimony: "Well, I decided that it would be good for the quality of my work to invite God along."

Later still, that same friend asked Kevin to pray for his father when he was dealing with a problem. Somewhere down the road, who knows how that simple act of daring will affect the office environment?

Bob worked as an up-and-coming executive for a large manufacturing organization. The company maintains plants throughout the world and in several major U.S. cities.

After around four years he was offered a promotion that would move the family to the Midwest for at least three years. "It's a sweet offer, Derek," he said as we teed off on the first hole of the company golf course. "But I'm not sure I'm going to take it."

"Why on earth not?" I asked.

"Well, as you know, we're pretty active in the church here. My girls will be in high school soon, and they have a supportive circle of church friends they're going to be with. As a family we're involved in the mission ministry team, and it feels as though our faith is just now getting into high gear after all these years.

"Bottom line, Derek"—he paused long enough to hit a long, floating slice and watch it disappear deep into the adjacent woods—"is that quality of life is about a lot more than money and position." He put a second ball on the tee and neatly hooked it into a pond. "My quality of life is more clearly defined than that."

So Bob went into his boss's office early the next week and said he was declining the offer. Forty years old, he understood that such a decision could very well signal the end of a promising career. He did something more, however, a step of daring that knocked my socks off. He shared the same sentiments with his employer that he had with me. He talked about his family; he talked about the life they enjoyed together at the church; and he shared openly—unselfconscious about his abiding faith in God.

That is what I call being courageous. Bob did not lose his job; in fact, his company eventually promoted him locally because it valued his integrity and personal work ethic so much. Not only that, but his speaking up turned out to be one more important element in a series of actions that led—over time—to a family-friendly shift in the corporate culture.

Paul offered some timely advice for the Christians in Corinth that could just as appropriately have been directed to North American men who are often forced to deal with a business climate that stands at odds with the principles and priorities of faith: "Keep alert, stand firm in your faith, be courageous, be strong. Let all that you do be done in love" (1 Cor. 16:13-14).

14   SO WHAT'S STOPPING US?

I do not call you servants any longer, because the servant does
not know what the master is doing; but I have called you friends,
because I have made known to you everything that I have heard
from my Father. You did not choose me but I chose you. And I
appointed you to go and bear fruit, fruit that will last.

—*John 15:15-16*

I'd like to bring our discussion to a close by issuing a simple challenge.

Are we willing to take the risk of stepping outside the limitations
of business as usual in order to live a life of deliberate Christian discipleship? Or, to put it another way, are we ready to embrace life in all
its fullness, and to live with the sense of purpose and promise that
stands against mediocrity and engages everything that God intended
for us when he sent Jesus to set us free?

Imagine Jesus himself, quite literally liberating us from vain and
empty lives. Imagine freedom from the pointlessness of investing our
time and applying our resources in pursuit of exactly the wrong kind
of treasure. Imagine independence from the kind of riches that will
never come close to bringing genuine satisfaction.

Remember what my friend Darrell said: "Let me get this straight. I'm
used to telling God what I want and then wondering if he's going to get
on board. Now you're suggesting I actually allow God to change me?"

Responding to Christ's imperative is critical if we intend to live
God's kind of wonderful life. Jesus said, "In this world you will have
trouble. But take heart! I have overcome the world" (John 16:33, NIV).
Dare to pray, and dare to read the scripture. Then dare to live.

I honestly believe that the real genius of this amazing adventure
that is Christian faith resides in the daring. Men of action, engaging
Christ's invitation to "follow me"; men who see their moment-by-
moment experience of daily life in terms of the opportunity vested in

a spiritual journey; men who risk stepping outside the malaise of the status quo in order to live a full-contact life of deliberate discipleship.

Daring suggests—and I know we have already discussed this in some detail—that what it means to be a Christian man these days necessarily involves coloring outside the lines. To be a Christian man is, essentially and unavoidably, to be countercultural.

Daring also means the practice of servant leadership in the context of our family; it means actively striving to be the presence of Christ in our workplace; and it means constantly reflecting on the opportunity and the imperative to serve.

Daring is not about WWJD (What would Jesus do?) so much as it is about WWJHMTD (What would Jesus have me to do?). It is not so much *The Purpose-Driven Life* as it is the Jesus-Driven Purpose.

I guess that, more than anything else, we have been talking about what it means to really live. After my friend Steve jumped out of that airplane and his parachute failed, he understood two things very clearly. One: Death is not really the end of our life; or rather, our life is much greater and more wonderful than simple physical existence. And two: Life is so precious that we do not want to waste a moment of our time by not really living.

I had an interesting experience one day when my own mortality helped me see life with sharper clarity. I had scheduled a day away from work so Rebekah and I could visit our attorney and finalize our wills. The documents had already been prepared, so we reviewed them together before signing with an old-fashioned fountain pen. We shook hands with the attorney, said good-bye, and climbed into my pickup truck.

I carefully placed our new wills on the seat between us, with the signature pages on top. The ink was still wet, and we didn't want the documents to smudge. I pulled away, turned immediately right, and approached the light that regulated traffic coming off the exit ramp from the interstate. I glanced up, thought about the best route to the coffee shop, and made a last-moment decision to turn left.

We had signed the new wills less than ninety seconds previously, and the ink was still wet when the fully loaded semi hit my driver's-side door square on at around forty-five miles per hour. All I remember is the sense of something being there and a disinterested curiosity that I could read the *I* for International on the truck's front grille so clearly. We were, I was told later in the vernacular of automobile wrecks, "T-boned."

Essentially, the driver's side of my little Nissan ceased to exist. My door had moved over on top of the gearshift, and my seat was—how should I say—neatly folded. Curiously, I was uninjured. Rebekah had a gash in her head, but we both went home from the emergency room that afternoon.

For some reason, all I could think about was the story Jesus told (Luke 12:16-21) about the man who spent his last day on earth making piles of all his stuff and rubbing his hands together in glee because he was so wealthy. "And I will say to my soul, Soul, you have ample goods laid up for many years; relax, eat, drink, be merry." I couldn't help but wonder if the way I spend my time gives any more evidence of the real Christ-life than that.

Bottom line: I want to be, as Jesus put it, "rich toward God."

Living as real men

Men like to see the fruits of their labors: "I built that"; "I closed that deal"; "I made that happen." The Bible clearly says that only the things that are done for God will last for eternity. A real man will focus on those things. Being Spirit-led, living a life of fullness—that's when God can break in and make a change.

Being a Christian man is all about cutting to the chase and focusing on what's important. It's about making a difference in terms of significance rather than getting caught up in what is run-of-the-mill and unproductive. Wandering through life misdirected, without understanding or even bothering to try to find out what is truly important, is the antithesis, I believe, of God's calling for men. The only way to be genuinely productive on an eternal scale is through making a firm connection with God. "Therefore be imitators of God, as beloved children, and live in love" (Eph. 5:1-2).

Last year I attended a significant college reunion. It was fun; I reconnected with a few really great people, and it was fascinating to catch up on the passage of so many interesting lives.

I couldn't help but think about the "University was the best time of my life" line we hear so often. So I was gratified to discover that most of the folk I talked with that weekend presented a different perspective. They told stories about rich experiences, positive communities of faith, committed family lives, and meaningful relationships.

College was a fun memory; nobody disputed that, but it turns out that *today* is the most consequential time we can ever engage. Our past experiences can be valuable building blocks for our lives; some are even cornerstones. But what will we choose to do with our todays and our tomorrows? The decisions we make will be some of the most important we ever face. Do we dare to choose to follow Jesus?

Desire, discipleship, devotion, and daring

My Men's Room Bible study group had a long conversation about some changes they might make in their lives if perchance they knew they only had a short while to live.

"I'd put my priorities in order," one man said.

"I'd spend more time with my children," another chimed in.

"I'd love my wife the way I know I should," someone else resolved.

Each man, after thinking for a few moments, pledged quite solemnly that he would take more deliberate steps to live out his Christian faith with courage, purpose, and conviction.

"I'd make sure it would be a lot easier for people to know that I follow Jesus," Eric said, speaking for pretty much every man there in the room.

"So what's stopping you?" I asked. "Why not today?"

In fact, now that I mention it, what's stopping any of us?

ACKNOWLEDGMENTS

Thanks a million to all the folk at Upper Room Books: Lynne Deming for believing from the get-go; Anne Trudel, my project manager; Marilyn Beaty for the initial referral; Jill Ridenour for her marketing savvy; Karen Duncan and Rita Collett for help with the details; and others on staff I'm sure I'll get to know.

Additionally, I want to express my gratitude to:

- every incarnation of The Men's Room, both at Trinity in Pensacola and First Presbyterian Church of Brandon.
- my other group—Rebekah, Ben and Lynn, Steve and JoEllen, Karin and David, Sandy, Christine, John and Lynn, David and Carrie, Stan and Carolyn.
- the original covenant group—Rebekah and Derek, Sandee, Margie, Paul and Katherine.
- Stephen Ministries and the ChristCare Series® folk in St. Louis.
- Jerry Noland.
- Tim and Kelly Black.
- two friends who have always encouraged: Gail Owens and LaNelle Pierce.
- the amazing family of faith who worships together at First Presbyterian Church in Brandon, Florida.

NOTES

CHAPTER 1: GOOD NEWS FOR MEN!

1. Michael Yaconelli, *Messy Spirituality: God's Annoying Love for Imperfect People* (Grand Rapids, MI: Zondervan, 2002).

CHAPTER 2: A ROUND DOZEN FLAT-OUT GUYS

1. The exact quotation from Pascal's *Pensées,* section #553, is, "Console thyself, thou wouldst not seek Me, if thou hadst not found Me." Available at http://www.ccel.org/ccel/pascal/pensees.viii.html.

CHAPTER 3: WHERE'S OUR TREASURE?

1. From "Spirit of the Living God." Words by Daniel Iverson, 1926; based on Acts 11:15.

CHAPTER 4: SETTING OUR MINDS ON THE THINGS OF THE SPIRIT

1. Stephen R. Covey, *The 7 Habits of Highly Effective People: Powerful Lessons in Personal Change* (New York: Simon & Schuster, 2004).

2. Words by Isaac Watts. Caedmon's Call, a contemporary Christian band, recorded this text as "I Boast No More."

CHAPTER 5: THE STRUCTURE OF A WELL-GROUNDED FAITH

1. Eugene H. Peterson, *A Long Obedience in the Same Direction: Discipleship in an Instant Society* (Downers Grove, IL: InterVarsity Press, 2000).

CHAPTER 12: WHAT DO WE DARE?

1. John Ortberg, *If You Want to Walk on Water, You've Got to Get Out of the Boat* (Grand Rapids, MI: Zondervan, 2001).

CHAPTER 13: LIVING AS IF FAITH ACTUALLY MAKES A DIFFERENCE

1. C. S. Lewis, *The Lion, the Witch and the Wardrobe* (New York: HarperCollins Publishers, 2004).

ABOUT THE AUTHOR

Derek Maul writes a weekly op-ed column that runs in local editions of the *Tampa Tribune*. His commentary and features have appeared in *Newsweek, USA Today,* the *Christian Science Monitor, Presbyterians Today, Guideposts,* and many other print and online publications. He is married to Rebekah, a Presbyterian pastor. They have two children, Andrew and Naomi.

Before becoming a full-time writer, Derek taught public school in Florida for eighteen years, including cutting-edge work with autistic children. He holds bachelor's degrees in psychology and education from Stetson University and the University of West Florida.

Derek is active in teaching at his church: adult Sunday school, small-group ministry, and a men's Bible study/spiritual formation group. He enjoys the outdoors, traveling, photography, reading, cooking, playing guitar, and golf.

Other Titles of Interest

Get Real Leader's Guide

Derek Maul offers practical suggestions for a ten-week study of *Get Real: A Spiritual Journey for Men*. The Leader's Guide can be used in a number of ways: with small groups of six to twelve men who meet and study together on a regular basis; with Sunday school or continuing education classes; with one or more friends as a conversational guide; as a Web-based interactive study, with a virtual group simultaneously addressing the same chapters and the same questions; or as an individual study companion.

ISBN 978-0-9924-6 • Paperback • 56 pages

Living Your Heart's Desire
God's Call and Your Vocation
by Gregory S. Clapper

Clapper helps people of any age who are struggling to put their faith and their work together in powerful and meaningful ways. He helps clarify what it means to have a calling from God and what it means to live out that calling. Rather than focusing on some formula on how to obtain the "job you were created for," Clapper maintains that it is more helpful to have a firm grasp of the theological understanding of work, calling, and human freedom. This book can help you lead a fulfilled and joyful Christian life, regardless of how you make money.

ISBN 978-0-9805-8 • Paperback • 128 pages

To order, call 1-800-972-0433
or visit us online at
www.upperroom.org/bookstore